ORGANIZING PARENT GROUPS

ORGANIZING PARENT GROUPS

A Structured Approach to Parent Involvement

By Gary B. Wilson, M.A.

Humanics Learning
Atlanta, GA USA

HUMANICS LEARNING

Organizing Parent Groups
A Humanics Learning Publication

© 2001 by Brumby Holdings, LLC

No part of this book may be reproduced or transmitted in any form or by any means, electronic or mechanical, including photocopying, recording, or by any information storage and retrieval system, without written permission from the publisher. For information, address Brumby.

Humanics Learning Publications are an imprint of and published by Humanics Publishing Group, a division of Brumby Holdings, LLC. It's trademark, consisting of the words "Humanics Learning" and a protrayal of a silhouetted girl, is registered in the U.S. Patent Office and in other countries.

Brumby Holdings, LLC
1197 Peachtree Street
Suite 533 Plaza
Atlanta, GA 30361

Printed in the United States of America

Library of Congress Card Number:
ISBN: 0-89334-239-4

Preface

For many years, Humanics Learning has concentrated heavily on ways to help child development programs increase the involvement of parents in education. With American education about to launch a new phase of its growth, it seems time to draw together some of the learning and lessons of the past. In keeping with this format, we have used our collective experience in working with child development programs and schools across the nation to develop this manual.

We appreciate the efforts of the many people who made contributions to the preparation of this manual, those who provided the illustrations and made valuable suggestions about the graphics and the layout, those who tested the many concepts with individual programs and helped with modifications.

The author alone assumes sole responsibility for the ideas and opinions expressed herein.

In the text of this work, school and child development program committees are used as examples of structures for establishing the parent program in your educational setting. The model used in this work is based on Head Start parent guidelines translated to be applied to broader education applications.

Table of Contents

Preface v

I. Parent Involvement 1

II. How Parents Can Participate 11

III. Making Participation Meaningful 23

IV. What the Parent Groups Can Do 31

V. The Parent Sub-Committee 37

VI. What Are Parents Interested In? 45

VII. Parent Involvement and the Child Development Director 53

VIII. Parent Involvement and the Staff 63

IX. The Parent Involvement Council and the Board of Directors 87

X. Help, Hints, and Concluding Thoughts 99

Appendix 101

Chapter I
Parent Involvement

QUESTIONS MOST OFTEN ASKED ABOUT PARENT INVOLVEMENT:

- **Why Have It?**
- **Is It Possible?**
- **What can parent involvement really do?**
- **Is it necessary?**
- **Does it make any difference?**
- **Is it possible to get parents involved in the program?**
- **Why is it so difficult?**
- **How can I get parents more interested?**
- **Can parent involvement really have an effect on children's education?**

This chapter will help you to examine these questions in greater detail. It will give you some answers. And where you may not yet have answers, it will suggest some ways you can start to get answers for yourself.

There has been much research in the past twenty-five years which shows that children whose parents are involved in the education process become better students.

IS PARENT INVOLVEMENT NECESSARY?

Why do we have parent involvement? Parent involvement is a proven technique for improving the quality of the educational experience for children. Parents must become involved as the children begin their educational experience whether it is at age one or age six. The parent involvement process should last as long as the children are in an educational program, whether it is a pre-school, day care, elementary school, high school, or another educational setting.

Every Program Must Have Effective Parent Participation.

We must continue to discover new ways for parents to become deeply involved in decision-making about the program and in the development of activities that they deem helpful and important in meeting their particular needs. Every child development program is obligated to provide the channels through which such participation and involvement can be provided for and enriched.

Parent involvement is a must. The child development programs and schools that have good parent involvement will be those which get money to grow and expand to better serve the needs of the children, parents, and the community.

What Can Parent Involvement Do?

We have observed several good reasons for parent involvement. Right now, you may have several reasons of your own for wanting parents to become involved. Let's look at the following questions about what you can accomplish with your job.

WHAT CAN I DO?

Please circle "likely" or "unlikely" after each statement, according to what you believe you and the Parent Involvement Program are likely or unlikely to accomplish.

I can . . .

1. Help the parents to be better parents. *Likely Unlikely*

2. Help the staff to do a better job with the children. *Likely Unlikely*

3. Help the children to have more fun and learn more. *Likely Unlikely*

4. Help the program to get money for special events. *Likely Unlikely*

5. Help to unite the community and bring about improvements such as better lighting, better roads, and better educational facilities. *Likely Unlikely*

Did you think these were all possible? They are. Look at each of these ideas in detail.

Parent Involvement Can:

1. Help the parents to be better parents.

You will do this if you can bring the staff and parents together. Early childhood educators can teach the parents things about how children learn, how they grow, what foods they should eat, and how they can continue to learn at home. Parents will learn more about how to help their children and will therefore be better equipped to handle their roles as the primary educators.

2. Help the staff to do a better job with the children.

You will do this when you help the staff to talk with parents about real problems and issues with the children. The staff will learn more about each child and will be able to give him or her better care, counseling and help.

3. Help the children to develop a positive learning environment.

You can make this happen by bringing parents and staff together to talk about the individual strengths and weaknesses of each child. The parents will learn more about how to help their children at home, and the staff will know more about how to help each child at the school or center.

4. Help the program to get money and to increase the quality of education.

You will play a big part in whether your community will continue to have a quality educational facility. Communities with strong Parent Involvement Programs and good parent participation are the most likely to receive money for increased child development programs.

5. Help to unite the community and bring about improvement and change.

You will be doing this when you bring parents together in an effective group and give them the formal machinery to make themselves heard. An example of formal machinery would be a strong committee which makes decisions about the development program. When parents find that they can get together and make decisions about their children's education, they may want to get together for other community issues, as well.

In many ways you are very lucky. You can help people to lead better lives. You can play a big part in helping a lot of children get ahead in education and in life.

CAN THE PARENT COORDINATOR HAVE ANY INFLUENCE?

Getting parents involved is a tough job, but it can be done. Many staffs may have the wrong ideas about parents which get in the way of parent involvement. Here are some very common false statements I often hear:

"The parents from our community aren't interested in the program."

"The parents from our community don't care much about their children's education."

"The parents from our community don't see how their participation makes any difference."

"The parents from our community are too lazy to come out in the evenings to attend meetings."

"The parents from our community don't believe that we really mean it when we say we want their participation."

"The parents from our community don't have enough education to participate in the affairs of an educational program."

"The parents from our community don't know how to go about participating or where the child development program wants them to help."

"The parents from our community never have much opportunity to talk about their children during the meetings because we always need to talk about other business. They don't come to meetings because they don't care about those things, their only real interest is their children."

What do you believe? How many of these statements do you feel are true? The following short stories may help you find out. Test yourself. Read each case study carefully. At the end you'll find questions and some answers to choose from.

Case Study 1

The Jones' little boy Tommy, age 4, attended school in a typical setting. Tommy's father seldom came to parent meetings, and when he did come, he had little to say. The Parent Coordinator felt that he had little interest in the program. One day Tommy came home with his shirt torn. He told his father that the teacher had hit him and torn his shirt.

What do you think Mr. Jones did?

A. Told Tommy he was a bad boy for making the teacher hit him.
B. Laughed and told Tommy he deserved to be hit.
C. Went as quickly as possible to the school to find out what happened and to learn if the story was true.
D. Paid no attention and did nothing.

Case Study 2

One day the Parent Coordinator from a typical school setting received a telephone call from her Director. He said that a very important visitor from the Federal Government was going to visit the school and wanted to meet with the parents. The Coordinator told all the parents that an important visitor was coming and that they should come to the meeting.

What do you think probably happened on the night of the meeting?

A. Very few parents showed up for the meeting.
B. An unusually large group of parents went to the meeting.
C. A moderate-sized group showed up.

For Case Study 1, you probably circled item C: "Went as quickly as possible to the school to find out what had happened and to learn if the story was true." For most parents in school communities, this is probably what would happen.

What does it mean? It means that parents do care about what happens to their children. It means that whenever they think their child is being harmed, they will try to do something about it immediately. It means that parents probably do not participate more because they are satisfied with the job you are doing and don't believe they could help make it more successful.

For Case Study 2, a number of Parent Coordinators have been surprised that the answer is almost always item B: "An unusually large group of parents went to the meeting." In most all child development centers and schools, parents visit the facilities when they learn that an important visitor is coming.

What does this mean? It means that parents do care about their child development programs. They will show up for a meeting if they believe it will make a real difference.

These stories should remind us of some things we often forget when working with parents. Parents usually care more for their children than they do for themselves. They work long hours to support their children's educational needs, and many often tolerate unhappy marriages to provide a home. When parents genuinely believe their children's interest is at stake, they will make great sacrifices. You may be a parent. Is this true for you and your children?

If these beliefs are true, then, we can state some "Principles of Parent Involvement."

Principles of Parent Involvement

The **ABC**'s

A. Parents do care about their children. They will participate when they believe they are helping their children or are learning something which they believe will help them to be better parents.

B. Parents do care about their child development programs and want them to be successful. Parents will participate if they believe that their participation will make a difference in the community. Telling them it makes a difference will not make them believe it. They must feel it.

C. Parents are adults. They do not like sitting in meetings if they:

    1. Don't think they are being useful to the community.
    2. Don't believe they can contribute to the community.
    3. Are uncomfortable physically or emotionally.
    4. Think they are being treated like children.

They do not want to participate in "token" meetings. Telling them they are useful or can contribute, for example, will make little difference. They must feel it, believe it, and see it happen.

You can use these principles to achieve stronger participation in your child development program. You can use these principles to help parents involve themselves in the daily activities of your program. In this manual we will examine the ways we believe you can do this. But before we continue, you may want to pause for a brief review of what we have discussed so far.

Review

The Parent Coordinator's Job

What have you learned from this chapter? These questions may help you to organize your thoughts, so please, take a few minutes to write down your ideas.

Are these some of the things you thought you learned?

You have a significant and important job.
You can help child development programs to stay in operation.
You can help children to have better educational experiences.
You can help parents to be better parents.
You can help to improve your community.

This is what I hoped this chapter would show and, finally, here is what I hope you will learn about your own possibilities as a Parent Coordinator:

You do have influence in the child development program.
People outside of your facility care about parent involvement.
The program has guidelines and rules that can be used to help you do your job.

The skills and information obtained in this manual will help you to do a more effective job.

My Thoughts About Parent Involvement

_____

_____

_____

_____

_____

Chapter II
How Parents Can Participate

In this chapter we will do two things:

1. We will list all the major ways parents can be involved in the child development program.
2. We will show how the principles or parent involvement can help you to get parents involved.

WAYS PARENTS CAN PARTICIPATE

Parents can participate in a variety of ways. They can participate in formal activities and groups or in informal ways. One part of your job is to continuously think of ways to involve parents in your development program. The staff and the parents can also contribute new ideas.

Child Development programs contain formal groups and activities to involve parents. Some of these are:
The Classroom Comittee
The Child Development Program (School) Committee
The Volunteer Committee

Many programs have also found informal ways to involve parents. Some of these are:
Meetings with the teachers and other staff members.
Special projects for the children, such as field trips and community theater.
Special committees for issues such as school security, drugs, and students dress codes.

Which of these areas are important? Anything you can do to get parents meaningfully involved in your program is important. For example, your first concern would be with formal groups such as the School Committee and the School Council. You might want to implement a similar structure in your education program.

Let's discuss the purpose and functions of each of these groups.

The Classroom Committee

The Classroom Committee is primarily an advisory and helping committee. The Committee's purpose is to help the parents express their ideas about the programs that will best meet the needs of the children. It assists with the selection of the staff, the recommendation of new programs, and annual evaluations. The following is a list of the functions of the Classroom Committee. You may want to compare your opinion of what the committee's purposes and responsibilities should be with the actual guideline set forth by your center. You can do this by completing the following exercise.

Instructions: Circle the letter beside the function which you believe is correct.

The Classroom Committee:

1. a. May participate in recruiting and screening new staff;
   b. Tells staff members when they are not doing well;
   c. Fires staff;
   d. Decides menus;
   e. None of these.

2. a. Assists in the development of curriculum;
   b. Decides menus;
   c. Hires new staff, interviews;
   d. Appropriates the expenditure of funds;
   e. None of these.

3. a. Plans, conducts and participates in center activities for parents' night;
   b. Decides what supplies the center can buy;
   c. Review and makes recommendations about the curriculum;
   d. Decides menus;
   e. Hires new staff.

4. a. Approves the expenditure of center funds;
   b. Decides curriculum;
   c. Finds transportation;
   d. Hires staff;
   e. Assists staff in recruiting people and resources (for example, volunteers) to carry out activities.

5. a. Approves all decisions that affect the classroom;
   b. Recruits new staff;

c. Helps parents to find ways to get together and share common interests;
   d. Finds transportation for the children;
   e. None of these.

Answers: 1. a, 2. a, 3. a, 4. e, 5.c

The Parent Involvement Council

Let's look briefly now at the purpose of the Parent Involvement Council. This group has more power and influence than the Classroom Comittee. It is called a Parent Involvement Council because it makes use of the resources parents provide in helping to establish policies and make decisions about what the Child Development Program will do. Parents are not sole members of this group. The parents elect representatives from their Classroom Comittee to attend the council. There is no exact number of parent members, though a good rule of thumb is that at least 50% of this group should be parents. The others should be representatives from the community, public and private agencies and major community civic or professional organizations that have a concern for children. This group also has specific duties and responsibilities.

As you did before, take the following quiz to determine the functions of the Parent Involvement Council.

The Parent Involvement Council:

1. a. Approves or disapproves the goals of the program;
   b. Approves Child Development needs;
   c. Determines the location of the central office;
   d. Is responsible for developing plans to use community resources;
   e. None of these.

2. a. Is responsible for establishing a method of hearing and resolving complaints about the School;
   b. Must direct the daily operation of staff;
   c. Must select the children;
   d. Must welcome staff into home for home visits;
   e. None of these.

3. a. Has operating responsibility and annual evaluation of the center;
   b. Has responsibility for making major changes in the budget and work program while program is in operation;

    c. Hires and fires Director of the center;
    d. Hires and fires staff of the center;
    e. None of these.

4. a. Must approve or disapprove major changes in the budget or work program while program is in operation;
    b. Has no general responsibility to prepare funding requests for the proposed education program;
    c. May be consulted about the hiring or firing of the center Director;
    d. None of these.

5. a. Does not approve or disapprove the location of the classrooms;
    b. May be consulted about the daily operation of the program;
    c. Must be consulted about the criteria for admitting children to the School;
    d. Must be consulted about hiring and firing of staff;
    e. None of these.

Answers: 1. a, 2. a, 3. a, 4. a, 5. c.

As a Parent Coordinator, it's very important that you know exactly what your groups are for and what they can and cannot do.

Before reading this manual, you will want to know some of the basic responsibilities of the parent groups. The following is a brief review of the Classroom Comittee and the School Council.

If you already know this material, you may want to skip ahead to the next section of this chapter, "Getting Parents Involved."

The Classroom Committee

Membership: Parents whose children are attending the center. No staff member may serve on the Classroom Committee.

Purpose: To share information about the children with staff; to join other parents in planning activities and programs of benefit to themselves and the children; to gather information about the child development needs and community concerns vital to the action of the Program Council; to assist staff in delivering the best possible program for children.

Some Functions And Responsibilities:

Here are some examples of how Classroom Committees have implemented their functions and responsibilities.
(Additional functions and suggestions for achieving them can be found in Appendix B.)

1. Provide ideas and opinions about the educational needs of the community. At monthly meetings, parents may plan to survey the educational needs of their neighborhood or visit other centers.

2. Provide ideas and opinions about the goals of the center. Inform the community about what is possible and available in the center. Inform Parent Involvement Council about how the Classroom Committee is meeting or not meeting the needs of the neighborhood.

3. Recommend community resources that are available to the center. List the resources that are known to parents and could be helpful to the classroom and center at large. Determine if other community resources are needed. Invite all resource contacts to the Class parents meeting to discuss how you feel they could be helpful.

4. Provide ideas and opinions for the recruitment of children. Discuss who may need to be in special programs. What problems should be considered? How should vacancies be advertised? Take recommendations about how children are to be recruited to the Parent Involvement Council.

5. Work with Classroom staff to carry out daily activities program. At the meeting develop a schedule of volunteers to assist in the classrooms. Survey the parent group for special talents: musical, story telling, building, etc.

6. Plan, conduct and participate in programs and activities for parents and staff. At meeting discuss what parents like to do best. Choose some of these ideas and see if they can be implemented.

7. Participate in recruiting and screening of employees. Select a personnel committee to interview and recommend applications for employment in your center.

The School Council

Membership: Members must be parents whose children are in the School. The other members are approved by those parents. They may be people from the community who have something special to offer the School. For example, one such person might be chairman of the community's School Board.

Purpose: To give parents and representatives of the community a chance to influence and shape the educational resources so that the council fulfills the community needs. This group has the responsibility for contacting resources within the community that will benefit the program. In addition, the Council can serve as another important voice to local, state and federal agencies about the communities wants and needs.

Duties and Responsibilities: You will find that some of the duties of the School Council are very different from those of the Classroom Comittee. The School Council has special and unique responsibilities.
(Additional functions and suggestions for achieving them are to be found in Appendix B)

Planning:
1. Provide ideas and opinions about the educational needs of the community.

2. Recommend goals of the center program.

3. Recommend plans to use the community resources.

4. Recommend plans to recruit children.

General Administration:
1. Recommend the services that the local educational agency will provide to the center.

2. Take full responsibility for establishing a method for hearing and resolving community complaints and concerns about the center.

3. Give advice and opinions about the center standards for acquiring space, equipment, and supplies.

Evaluation:
1. Participate in evaluating the Child Development Program during the program year.

2. Determine special needs for special programs.

That's a long list and a lot of responsibility! You can see that if these Committees and Councils do their jobs, the parents will have a real voice in how their schools and centers are run, which children are admitted, how and what the children are taught, and who teaches them.

Just for fun, stop and think for a minute what would happen if the parents in your community were actively involved in these ways. Let your imagination go.

Here's one hope. The parents would find that they are capable of performing these tasks. They would find that there is strength in numbers and unity. They might want to turn to look at other problems in their community beyond the center. They might even begin to solve other community problems together.

That might sound like a dream, but being a good parent is a very realistic dream. Before it can come true, however, you must get down to the nitty-gritty of helping parents get together to form strong Councils and Committees and to take an active part in their center.

GETTING PARENTS INVOLVED

Let's begin by looking at how you can get parents involved. First, let's look again at the three principles of Parent Involvement.

Parents do care about their children.
They will participate when they believe they are helping their children or are learning something which they believe will help them to be better parents.

What does this mean for you? It means that if parents have not become involved in the program, they do not see how their participation will help their children. And they probably do not see how it will help them.

Perhaps now you are thinking that "it's different" in your program, that there are special circumstances in your community. That is very unlikely. You may be saying, "We tell them over and over again how important their participation is, they should know!"

If you will stop and think for a moment, you may recall that you haven't changed many of your beliefs or attitudes simply because somebody told you they were wrong, or that there were better ones. You don't buy a car, or instance because someone on television says it's a good buy. You might go and look at it for that reason, but you want to drive it and have a good experience with it. It's the same for parents. They need to have an experience in which they find that involvement does help them and the children.

So, the importance of our first "principle" of parent involvement is that Parent Coordinators must find ways for parents to have experiences which:
a. help their children; and
b. help them as parents.

Parents do care about their centers and want them to continue. Parents will participate if they believe that their participation will make a difference to the classroom and to their children.

To test whether this principle was true, we asked a number of parents the following question:

Do you think your center needs your opinions, ideas and help to be an effective center? Does the classroom need these things from parents?

Here are some possible answers to the questions. See if you can guess what the parents actually said. Circle the number you feel that parents from your program might give. You may select as many answers as you think they might give.

Possible Answers
Select and Circle the correct items you think might be said by parents:

1. The parents know more about their children and how they should be taught than anyone else.

2. The Parents can give staff help and guidance about what the children need to learn.

3. The staff are professionals. They have more education than we do. They are experts. We can't tell them anything they don't already know.

4. We parents have a lot of good ideas which could really help the Child Development Center.

5. We don't know anything about how to run a Child Development Center.

6. We don't have enough time to learn all about our child's education. We couldn't give many good ideas.

7. The staff doesn't want our opinions and ideas.

8. The staff and Director need our ideas and opinions because the program was established to be a cooperative effort between parents and staff.

Obviously, the way parents would answer these questions is a matter of opinion and will change from community to community. If you circled answers 1, 2, 4, and 8, you might be right for your community. But for most communities, the parents would give answers like 3, 5, 6, and 7.

If parents don't think their participation is really necessary, will they participate? We don't think so. But if they felt they could really do something for the school and that the staff really wanted them, would they participate? We think they would.

This means that if you are to have parent involvement, you will need to help the parents to really learn something they feel they need to know or really benefit from parent involvement; and feel that their contribution to school is important, wanted and necessary.
There is one more thing you can do. This has to do with the third principle we looked at before.

Parents are adults and must be treated like adults. They do not like to sit around in meetings if they don't think they are useful, if they don't think they can contribute anything, if they are uncomfortable physically or emotionally, and if they feel that they are being treated like children.

Does your Child Development Center ever violate or ignore the third principle? Here are some things to look for:

1. Does your program ever ask parents to come to meetings where there are only children's chairs or desks to sit in?
2. Does it have parents come to meetings where the room is too large, too small, too warm or too cold, or where it is difficult to hear what is being said?
3. Does it have parents come to meetings where they are asked to talk about trivial matters which are not directly related to education, such as who will bake cookies or who will drive the cars on the next field trip?
4. Does it ask parents to come to a meeting for a ninety minute lecture on how to participate in a meeting?

Many schools are guilty of putting parents in these types of uncomfortable situations. And there are many more ways a program can violate this third principle. Can you think of some from your own experience? The next time one of your Classroom Comittees is planning a meeting, take a close look and see if it is violating any one of these three principles. You might ask some other staff members to do this with you.

We've looked at the three basic principles of parent involvement and what they mean. In the next chapters we will begin looking at ways:

1. To help parents to have a good experience, to feel that they or their children can be better off because of their involvement;
2. To help parents see how they can participate and that their participation is important and necessary;
3. To help parents feel comfortable and that they are treated with respect during their meetings.

Chapter III
Making Participation Meaningful

Your job is getting parents involved. Our first chapter presented some principles for parent involvement, things you must remember as you go about your daily job. But what exactly should that daily job be? Principles and ideas are fine, but what do you do on a day-to-day basis to involve parents? This chapter presents a system and specific suggestions for day-to-day work.

When you begin to plan for parent involvement, you will need to think about two things:

1. The content: Which areas parents can influence, the areas in which they can make decisions, and the kinds of activities they might do together.

2. The process: How parents can participate most easily and effectively. Which are the parents most likely to have time for: monthly meetings, weekly meetings, mail votes, and so on. You might call this the 'vehicle' for participation. For example, just as you car is your vehicle for getting to the supermarket, you must have a vehicle for achieving total parent involvement.

ESTABLISHING THE PROCESS FOR PARTICIPATION

Let's look at the process, or vehicle, of parent participation.

Whenever you decide to go to the supermarket, you start looking for a way to get there. You have several options: your own car, if you have one; a friend's car; a bus; or even a taxi. Of course, you want to find the quickest, most convenient, and most enjoyable method available to you.

Usually, you don't give much thought to a problem like this. You figure it out quickly, almost subconsciously. Instead, you're usually thinking about what you want to buy when you get to the market. But if getting to the market were more difficult, you would spend more time deciding how to get there, and you would probably go a lot less often.

One of the biggest problems with parent participation is that we spend most of our time thinking about what we want to do with the parents or what we would like them to do, and too little time helping them find a 'vehicle' with which to do it. This would be like spending all our time planning our shopping list and forgetting to plan how we will get to the store. So the parents are left stranded. They know they are supposed to do something, but they don't know exactly what to do or how to do it.

You're probably wondering if that is true for your program. Maybe you're thinking, "We could have participation if the parents would only come to our meetings." Let's examine this statement.

Parent participation means that at least one parent from each household is involved in the curriculum and activities of the school. All schools would like to have both parents as often as possible. For most schools, this means thirty to one hundred parents or more!

Suppose fifty parents came to a meeting. How many could participate meaningfully in an hour-and-a-half or two hours? How much debate could there be? How much work and decision-making could get done?

Very little! All of us know that meetings are a very difficult way to do business, study issues, and make decisions. It takes great skill and much planning to make a large meeting work. What is the maximum size meeting in which you think you can do productive work? We would say three to five people but no more than ten.

Now let's look at how parents are usually asked to participate. Look at the 'vehicle' we use for participation in most schools. It is a monthly meeting which all parents are asked to attend. Often, it is held far from their homes and at night when many are tired from a day's work. The meeting usually takes place in children's classrooms where the only place to sit is in children's chairs.

In this situation, the number of parents who attend is unlikely to be as great as it would be if the circumstances were more appropriate. There will always be some who will participate because they like the chance to socialize with their friends or because they want to help. But most will simply say, "I'm going to stay home. We're not going to get anything done anyway, so let's do something else tonight."

Why do they react this way? Let's remember one of our principles: parents will participate if they believe the can contribute something. They won't participate much when they don't believe they can do anything meaningful.

So, one important reason most parent programs do not work is simply because they fail to create effective ways for parents to participate. If you are going to have good parent participation, you must first set up the vehicle which will make it possible for parents to make a meaningful contribution. You cannot do this by yourself. You will need approval and support from all of the staff. We will talk about that in later chapters. Let's look first at a system for parent participation which will give parents a real opportunity to participate.

An Overview of the New System

The next few pages will outline a completely new approach to parent involvement. You may find it easier to understand if you have a picture of the total system before you begin. The ideas are compatible with most schools.

This program has three basic parts:
Parent Sub-Committees
The Classroom Committee
The school (School) Council

A picture of these parts looks as follows:

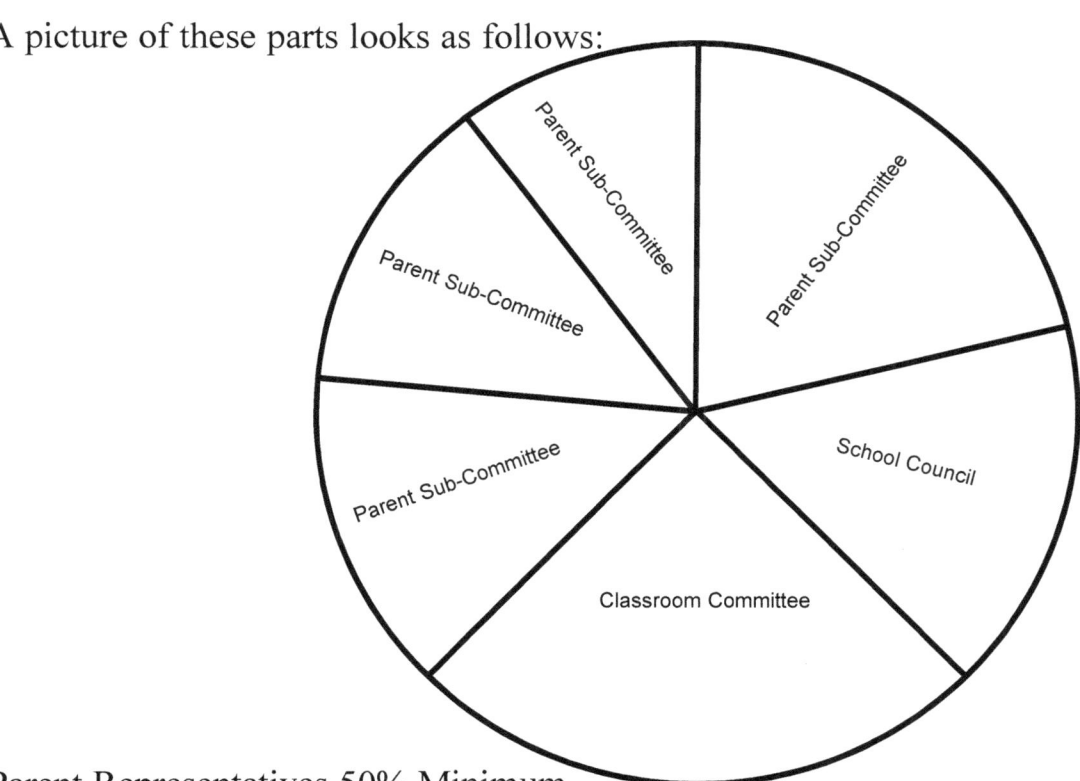

Parent Representatives 50% Minimum
Community Leaders and Representatives 50% Maximum

What's different? The Parent Sub-Committee! A group consisting of all parents of a classroom is too large for everyone to participate in at one time. If it meets only once a month, many parents will be unable to attend on the night chosen. For some, perhaps a majority, transportation is an important factor in their decision not to attend.

What would you do if someone gave you a piece of pie that was too big to eat? You'd cut it into smaller pieces. That's exactly what we're suggesting you do with you Classroom groups. Just as states and cities are divided into counties and precincts so that more people can participate in choosing their government and making laws, your program can achieve more participation by dividing parents into smaller, more workable groups.

When individual parents feel they are a part of a smaller group of people who know each other, more will participate. When each parent feels he or she is in a group small enough for everyone's individual voice to be heard, more parents will participate. The essence of the plan you are about to look at is that every parent is a part of a small, local group of parents he or she knows well.

Step One:
Organize Parents Into Local Groups

Who Is In Each Group And How Many?

Your first step is to organize the parents of each of your classrooms into small groups of between five and eight parents. You can do this by geographic location or by classroom. If you are in a rural area, you may find it better to organize the parents who live closest together into small groups even though their children may be in different classrooms. If you are working with an urban program, you will probably find that it will be better to divide parents by classroom.

Try to organize your groups so that the number does not exceed ten parents. The best number is between three and six.

The typical classroom will have between three and six these small groups. These groups will be called Parent Sub-Committees.

WHERE THE GROUPS MEET:

The Parent Sub-Committee will meet in places which are convenient for each group. Probably, each Parent Sub-Committee will want to meet at some member's house where they can be comfortable, but they might choose to use a local church, school, library or other facility.

WHEN THE GROUPS MEET:

Each of the Parent Sub-Committees must meet at least once a month. They should try to meet between the first day and the tenth day of the month, for example, a group would meet at the time of its choice between the dates of January 1 and January 10.

WHAT THE GROUPS DO:

These will be the most basic groups for your Parent Program. They are individual pieces of your "pie." In each of these groups, the parents will discuss issues and questions relevant to the program and their children. For example, they will discuss such subjects as staff and budget, and will make recommendations for the Classroom Comittee.

STEP TWO:
SELECT REPRESENTATIVES TO THE CLASSROOM COMITTEE

Each Parent Sub-Committee will select two representatives to sit on the Classroom Comittee. One of these parents will be the regular representative. The other will be an alternate. The alternate will attend Classroom Comittee meetings whenever the chief representative cannot attend. The regular representative for the Classroom Comittee may also be the Chairman of the Parent Sub-Committee. Of course, any parent may attend at any time, but the Parent Sub-Committee representatives or the alternates must promise to attend.

STEP THREE:
HOLD A MEETING OF THE CLASSROOM COMITTEE

Who Is On It And How Many?:

The Classroom Comittee will now be composed of the representatives selected by the Parent Sub-Committees. It will usually have between twelve and twenty members, depending on the size of your class and how many Parent Sub-Committees have been formed.

WHERE THE CLASSROOM COMMITTEE MEETS:
The Classroom Comittee probably will want to meet at the school or wherever the parents regularly meet.

WHEN THE CLASSROOM COMMITTEE MEETS:
The Classroom Comittee will meet between the eleventh and the twentieth day of each month. For example, in January it would meet some time between January 11th and 20th.

WHAT THE CLASSROOM COMMITTEE DOES:
The duties and responsibilities of the Classroom Comittee were briefly listed in Chapter II. The Classroom Comittee will perform the duties outlined in the manual. In a later chapter, we will show you how you can help the Classroom Comittee to fulfill all its responsibilities.

STEP FOUR:
SELECT REPRESENTATIVES TO THE SCHOOL COUNCIL

During the first meeting, the Classroom Comittee must select at least two representatives for the School Council. Both of these representatives may attend each of the Parent Involvement Council meetings, or they may decide to have one person be the regular representative and the other person be the alternate.

STEP FIVE:
THE PARENT INVOLVEMENT COUNCIL MEETS

Membership:
The rule for determining membership of the Parent Involvement Council is roughly half and half. The Council is composed of at least 50% parents of children in the program and no more than 50% representatives of the community. The parent representatives, as we have said, are chosen by the Classroom Comittee. The community representatives might include business, school and government officials of the community.

WHERE THE PARENT INVOLVEMENT COUNCIL MEETS:
The members of the School Council or the chairman will decide where the Council meets.

When The Council Meets:

The Parent Involvement Council will meet between the twenty-first and thirty-first days of each month. Now you can see the complete schedule for the meetings of all the groups:

January 1 - 10 Parent Sub-Committees Meet
January 11 - 20 Classroom Committee Meets
January 21 - 31 Parent Involvement Council Meets

Let's review all the pieces of the structure we have formed. You have divided all the parents of the program into small groups call Sub-Committees. These groups meet in the first ten days of each month and make recommendations and decisions about the program's effectiveness. After these groups have met, their representatives attend a Classroom Committee Meeting between the eleventh and twentieth days of the month. At this meeting, the representatives of all the parents get to make their recommendations and decisions based on the meetings they have had in individual Parent Sub-Committees. Finally, after the Classroom Committees have met, the School Council will meet during the last ten days of the month and make their decisions based on the recommendations that have come to them through the Classroom Comittee and the Parent Sub-Committees.

You have just completed one of the most difficult parts of this manual. You may also find you have to read it carefully more than once before it is completely clear.

This plan is based on some assumptions about people: when they are most likely to participate in group activities and under what circumstances. You can test whether you agree with these assumptions by answering the following simple quiz:

ASSUMPTIONS ABOUT PARENT INVOLVEMENT

Circle T if you think the statement is true and F if you think it is false.

1. People are most likely to participate freely in groups in which they know the other members well. **T   F**

2. People are most likely to participate freely in groups in which they have a chance to make their point and explain it. **T   F**

3. when groups become larger than eight or ten people, it is often difficult to speak freely or to have coherent, informal discussions. **T   F**

4. When people can meet in comfortable, familiar circumstances, they are more likely to participate in a group's business. **T   F**

5. Individuals are most likely to get involved and interested in a group when they believe that they personally can have an impact on the group. **T   F**

6. To have effective participation, it is necessary to divide groups of people into small enough units so that individuals feel that their participation is meaningful. **T   F**

7. Groups must be structured so that each person has time to express his or her ideas. **T   F**

Did you circle all these statements as true? If so, you agree with the assumptions behind this approach. Generally speaking, each of these statements is true. If you believe that some are false, perhaps you are thinking of a particular instance which, for some reason, is an exception. Or perhaps you should stop and re-examine some of your ideas about groups. Try to think about the times when you have found it easiest and most productive to participate in a group. Then think about some of the times when you have found it most difficult or least satisfying to participate.

Now if you go back and read the questions again as statements, you will see that these are seven basic reasons why we believe you must divide the parents in your community into Parent Sub-Committees of fewer than ten members in order to have effective parent participation. List things that have worked for you in increasing parent involvement.

Chapter IV
What The Parent Groups Can Do

MAKING PARTICIPATION MEANINGFUL

In Chapter III, we observed that to achieve meaningful parent involvement, you must think about two things:

1. The content of the involvement - what parents can have a voice in, the areas in which they can make decisions, and the kinds of things the different parent groups can do.
2. The process—how parents can participate and the ways they can do it.

In the last chapter, we studied the vehicle for parent involvement. This chapter will present the same concepts and tools to help you with the content.

THE PARENT GROUPS AND THEIR FUNCTION

The structure that we have recommended is this manual describes three groups for the parent involvement structure for the school. Again, the ideas are compatible with the regulations of most programs. These three groups each have some unique functions or special things they can do. You will want to take advantage of these possibilities.

One unique role of the Sub-Committee is that it can be the group that helps staff and parents share information. In this group, for example, parents can learn what is being taught and how to follow through at home. They can share information about their children with that the staff may use for planning and teaching. In Chapter VII, you will see how you can get the staff to develop some lists. You might use such a list to make this group a meaningful link in the parent involvement program.

The Classroom Committee has several unique functions. One is to be the group in which parents can talk about the things that affect the school and the community which it serves; things such as how to raise money for special needs in the school, drug awareness, parent night programs, panels on violence in the school or neighborhood, and discussions with the agencies in the community about the needs of the children.

This group is also the funnel for information to the parents. For instance, this group should learn about what is happening with the Parent Involvement Council and report that to the separate Classroom Comittees. It is also where the Council representatives learn what the special concerns of the parents are and pass those on to the School Council.

The special function of the School Council is to provide a formal structure through which parents can participate in the policy-making and operation of the program. This group has the greatest power. Its job is to represent the wishes and feelings of the parents.

If you are going to help these different groups to carry out their responsibilities, you will probably want to develop some kind of "flow chart" specifying their duties, roles, and schedule of activities and deadlines.

Here is an example of such a chart:

Suggested Method For Planning Each Group's Structure

FIRST MONTH

First ten days:
Sub-Committee
Form, select Classroom Comittee representatives. Meet staff, discuss questions about children. Set volunteer calendar. Discuss any special problems that may exist at this time (security, drugs, before and after school programs).

Second ten days:
Classroom Committee
Select Parent Involvement Council representatives. Discuss reports of Sub-Committees. Make recommendations to Parent Involvement Council on action taken to comply with special conditions. Set some goals for school activities or parent programs.

Third ten days:
Parent Involvement Council
Select officers, make decisions about special problems in the school. Hear Class reports. Discuss desired community representation.

SECOND MONTH

First ten days
Sub-Committee
Review School Council minutes. Discuss ideas for school-wide parent program. Share thoughts about children's first month's experiences. Suggest community representatives for Parent Involvement Council.

Second ten days
Classrooom Committee
Discuss reports of Sub-Committees, make recommendations to Parent Involvement Council on action taken regarding special problems in the school. Finalize parent night plans. Recommend community representatives to Council.

Third ten days
Parent Involvement Council
Take action on special issues. Review Classroom Comittee reports. Decide on community representatives. Hear staff reports on progress of program to date.

This is just a sample chart. Naturally, you will want to adapt this chart and timetable to your program's particular needs and schedules. It is very important that you make some kind of flow chart. Without it, you can almost be sure that some part of your program or timetable will get lost.

How The Parent Coordinator Relates To The Parent Groups

We haven't said much about how you should behave or what your specific role within these groups should be. We won't. You must decide what is appropriate for your program. But we can give you some help in thinking about your role.

As a parent involvement coordinator, you will find that you are often asked to help others develop program ideas and respond to guidelines established by your program. You know that there are many ways you can assist, depending on how closely involved you can or want to be. For example, you could take over and direct the process by delegating responsibility to your staff and parent groups and by providing them with necessary information. Or you might simply act as a "parent consultant," helping others to think through what they are doing. This role requires that you maintain a delicate balance between being too involved and not involved enough.

What do we mean by "too involved?" The answer to this question varies from community to community, and perhaps from school to school, but here's a way you can check your degree of involvement. Take a moment to respond to these questions:

Parent Involvement Scale

1. Do parents refer to the parent program as:
   a. yours
   b. theirs

2. Do parents express their own ideas when planning the program or do they rely on your information?
   a. yours
   b. theirs

3. When work is to be done, do parents look to you or do they take the responsibility themselves?
   a. you
   b. themselves

4. When there is writing to be done (meeting announcements, letters to other agencies, etc.) who does the writing?
   a. you
   b. them

5. Whose ideas do parents feel are better and more creative?
   a. yours
   b. theirs

Your answers should give you some idea of your involvement.
Your Score: 1. a b   2. a b   3. a b   4. a b   5. a b
Their Score: 1. a b   2. a b   3. a b   4. a b   5. a b

What, on the other hand, are the things that would suggest to you the need for more involvement? Again, answers vary, but there are ways to determine "too little" involvement. Mark you answers to these statements.

1. Parents feel you are just a P. I. "staff person" for whom they must produce information and that you do not understand why the information is needed.
   a. true
   b. false
2. You do not understand why parent involvement is an important part of any school.

a. true
   b. false

3. You do not understand what needs parent involvement will meet in the community.
   a. true
   b. false

4. You cannot talk to the parent leadership openly with trust and candor.
   a. true
   b. false

Hopefully, most of your answers were false. If not, it's time to re-evaluate how you and others view your position and take steps to change these views.

The parent involvement coordinator's role as we have described it allows you to create a partnership between parents and staff. The partnership is not entirely equal. In some respects, you have the power to say "yes" or "no." Your actions have great significance and impact with the parent groups. This means you will want to take care to insure that "what you want is what you get." In other words, you want to be sure that parents see you the way you want to be seen.

Helpful Hints

Here are some suggestions for insuring that you are perceived in the way you want to be.

It is helpful if you...
1. Behave in ways that enable parents and staff working with you to trust you and feel comfortable offering constructive criticism.
2. Allow yourself to be flexible and encourage cooperation between others.
3. Work with others on explorations of programs as well as on problem-solving.
4. Listen to parent concerns and take them seriously.
5. Offer your expertise when appropriate.

Chapter V
The Parent Sub-Committee

ORGANIZATION AND FUNCTION

Dividing The Parents By Classroom Or Geography

Your first decision must be whether you will divide the parents in your program by classroom or by geography. If possible, you should try to divide them by classroom. Here is why:

1. Parents who are divided by classroom will have children who all have the same teachers and aides.
2. Parents who are divided by classroom will have children who are all receiving the same curriculum.
3. Because parents who are divided by classroom will have children who are receiving the same curriculum and who have the same teachers and aides, they will have more issues, concerns, and questions in common.

But how do you decide? Your first concern must be for the convenience of the parents. If they must drive long distances to a meeting or if they must take long bus rides (particularly in the evening), they will not be as likely to come to meetings. They will certainly want to schedule fewer meetings.

Therefore, in rural areas you may find it is better to help parents to form sub-committees based on geographic location.

To give you an example of what we mean, Figure V-1 is a diagram of a rural county with a Parent Involvement Program. In this case, parents are scattered throughout the county. It would not make much sense to organize them by classrooms. But it would be possible to organize five sub-committees by geography. According to this map, you would have the following five sub-committees:

MOBILE COUNTY

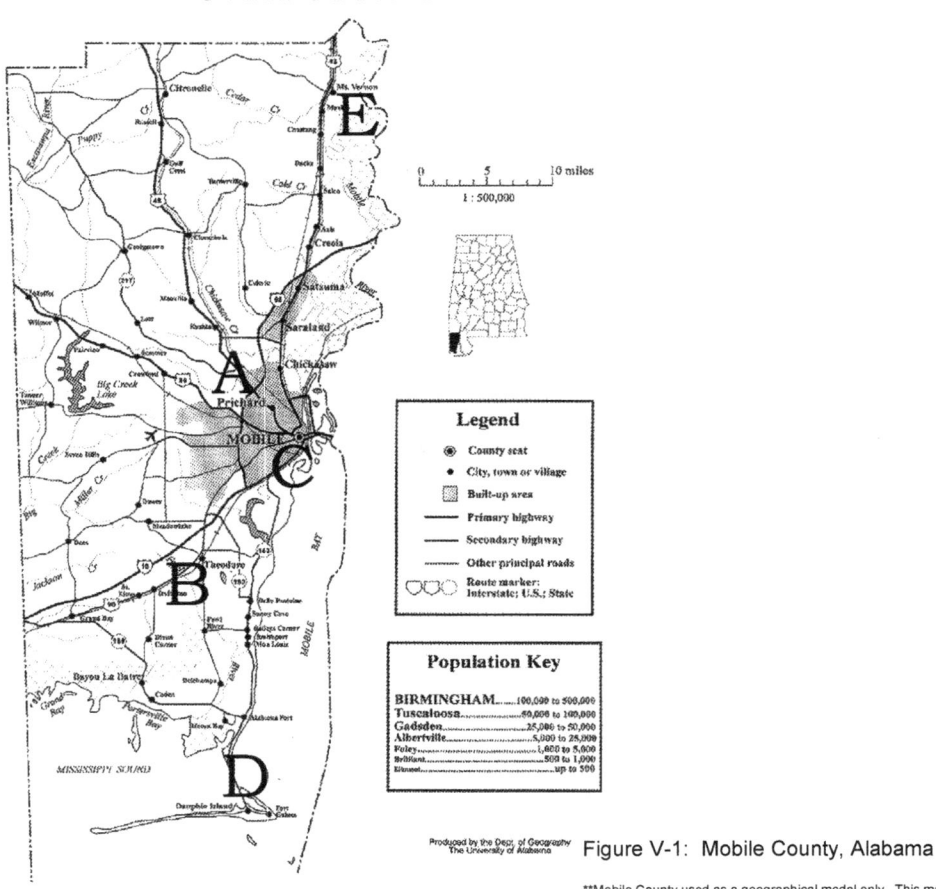

Figure V-1: Mobile County, Alabama

**Mobile County used as a geographical model only. This map is not intended to represent sub-committees that exist now or in the past.

Sub-Committee A: Prichard Sub-Committee
Sub-Committee B: Theodore Sub-Committee
Sub-Committee C: Mobile Sub-Committee
Sub-Committee D: Dauphin Island Sub-Committee
Sub-Committee E: Mt. Vernon Sub-Committee

When organizing Parent Sub-Committees, Keep the following ideas in mind:
1. Never let a group become larger than twelve if you can possibly avoid it. Remember your divisions are by household anyway; so if both parents in three or four families decided to attend a meeting that would double the group's size.
2. There is no set number of parents who may attend beyond the general recommendations of no more than twelve and no fewer than four. Thus, depending on your community, you might set up Sub-Committees of five, six, seven, eight, or nine parents.
3. Try to group your Sub-Committees around one central location; a town, community center or church, for example.

BEFORE THE PROGRAM BEGINS

You have decided the best way to divide up the parents in your community. Now you must inform the parents of your suggestions and help to see that the groups get organized.

The best and easiest time to do all this pre-planning is before school begins. The following plan us based on this fact, but you can still follow much of this plan even if your school year has already begun.

Here is a word of caution worth repeating. Before you contact any parent or begin to set up any meetings for parents, you must get the support of your Program Director and the staff. We will go into this more specifically in Chapters VII and VIII.

But first, the parents. Let us show you a sample orientation for parents designed to help you in two ways:

1. It will give you ideas on how to inform parents about your program.
2. It will help you to modify your system by providing you with valuable parent input.

STEP ONE:
Assemble The Parents On Opening Day

On the program's opening day, at least one parent of each child in a class must come to the school. This is a time when you will have all the parents together. This is also a time when the parents will be most interested and most prepared to learn about the school. You will need at least two and a half hours to accomplish your orientation to the Parent Program.

STEP TWO:
Give a Brief Lecture on Parent Involvement

Probably most of the parents will have no idea what the Parent Involvement Program is about, or they will have only a vague idea. Therefore, you must provide them with a brief explanation of what parent involvement means and in what areas parents are expected to take an active role. You may also describe briefly the different groups which will be established for parent participation and how they will function. Your presentation will probably be more effective if you have also prepared some "flip charts"* or newsprint which you can point to as you speak.

You may feel that you are not the best person to give this talk. Perhaps your Program Director would like to do it. Perhaps there is someone else on the staff of the school or even the community Action Agency or other sponsoring agency who would be more appropriate. This is perfectly acceptable. In such a case, however, it is important that the Parent Involvement Coordinator is introduced to the parents and that they know who you are.

Remember, increased student achievement is directly related to parent participation in the classroom.

*Flip Charts or "newsprint" are 24 inch by 36 inch sheets of paper that are purchased at most school/office supply stores, teacher-parent stores, or paper stores.

STEP THREE:
Answer Questions Parents May Have About The Program

At this time, some parents may want to question you about what you have said. Or they may have other questions about their relationships to the staff and the program. Of course, it would be helpful if some of the other staff, particularly the Director, were present during this question and answer period. Whether other staff are present or not, however, here are some hints about how to make such a meeting go as smoothly as possible.

Meeting Hints

1. If you don't know the answer, say "I don't know." Do not make up answers. Take the person's name and say that you will find the answer and get back in touch with him or her. Then be sure to get back in touch, even if no answer was available.
2. Be open to criticism! If a parent seems critical or doubtful, listen carefully to his or her point of view.
3. Ask for suggestions, if appropriate, and say that these will be taken into consideration.
4. Avoid Arguments!

STEP FOUR:
Hand Out Prepared List Of Parent Sub-Committees

After the question and answer period, hand out to each of the parents a list of all the Sub-Committees with the names of parents in each committee.

You will probably find that some parents' names are not on the list. Try to put them in the appropriate Sub-Committee at this time if it is clear where they belong or ask them to find their nearest neighbor on the list and join his or her Sub-Committee. Or, if neither of these is possible, take the names and addresses of those who are not assigned and tell them to meet with you immediately following the session. Then work out an appropriate assignment. Be sure to get them quickly into one of the groups that is meeting so you can proceed to Step 5.

STEP FIVE:
Ask The Sub-Committees To Form Into Groups

Each Parent Sub-Committee should be assigned one staff member from the school. If you have divided the parents by classroom, then the appropriate staff member would be the teacher or aide working with the children of those parents. If you have divided the parents by location, then you may assign the Staff Liaison to the Parent Sub-Committee at random or on a geographic basis, having staff members work with the groups nearest their homes.

Note: The Staff members assigned to each group must point out to the parents that staff have no vote or influence in the group. They are there to consult and mediate only and the parents should feel free to ask them to attend or not to attend meetings.

STEP SIX:
Assign Your Sub-Committees The Following Tasks:

A. Introduce one another, learn where everyone lives, how many children they have in the program, their ages, where and what hours they work, etc.

B. Arrange for a time when everyone present can meet each month. Remember that the sub-committees must meet between the first and tenth days of each month, for example, between September 1st and 10th, October 1st and 10th, etc.

C. Arrange for a place which is convenient to all members. This could be a church, library, school or even the home of one of the parents in the group.

D. Arrange for a temporary Chairperson. This parent will be the person responsible for getting messages to the other parents in the sub-committee until a permanent Chairperson has been selected.

E. Ask each group to plan to report the results of this meeting to the rest of the group.

F. If the Staff Liaisons (the staff member assigned to each group) are present, ask each group to discuss his or her role.

STEP SEVEN:
Ask Each Group To Report

Be sure to record the date, time, and place each group has agreed upon for its next regular meeting.

STEP EIGHT:
Hand Out Any Necessary Materials

Parents are asked to participate in the development and activities of the program and review special problems. It might be appropriate at this point to hand out copies of the school Calendar to enable parents to begin discussing Parent Activities.

STEP NINE:
Wrap-Up Lecture

Close the session with a review of the purposes of each group. Be sure to point out that each of the groups must select one representative and one alternate for the Classroom Comittee. Discuss some of the functions of the Classroom Comittee and the Parent Involvement Council.

You may also want to tell each group who its specific Staff Liaison will be in the case that any Staff Liaisons were unable to attend orientation.

STEP TEN:
Follow-Up

Now is the point when you really become a Parent Coordinator. Your next steps must be to assure that these essential meetings occur. This is one of the must crucial times in your program.

You have your own style; and you will develop a follow-up plan to suit your own style, the size of your program, and your resources. Here is a general plan, however, which might save you some time or give your some ideas:

1. Develop a calendar for the sub-committee meetings.
2. Next, write in your calendar a reminder to notify the parents and the Staff Liaison three days in advance of the Sub-Committee meeting and be sure all agree to attend. (You may find you have to do some hard persuading of a few parents at this point.)

What is your opinion? Is it really necessary to contact each parent three days before these first meetings? If so, is it better to remind each parent in person, by phone, or by a mailed notice? Which would be the least likely to make a difference, if any?

Check One:

☐   By Phone

☐   In Person

☐   By Mail

Why did you answer the way you did?

Experience with these kinds of organizations suggests that the most effective way to insure attendance is to see each parent in person or at least talk to each parent on the telephone. Mailed notices may be ignored or not even read.

What about the questions of whether you should spend your time in this way. This will require a lot of time and effort on your part. Is it worth it?

Remember, this will be the first meeting of the parents. When they were at the school on opening day, they agreed to this meeting. But a lot was happening that day. Once they got home they forgot about it. Things came up and others got busy. Some may have thought about it and decided it wasn't a good idea.

So your job is to remind, persuade, and coach. You may even have to help arrange transportation for some parents. And if you can contact all the parents in advance of this meeting, you will help increase the attendance greatly. You will also show (and this is one of the most important things you can do) that you and your program care about these meetings.

THE FIRST MEETING OF THE PARENT SUB-COMMITTEES

Now, let's examine what the parents might do during the first meeting. There are some important items of business which must be transacted. You can help insure that this is done by preparing a typed agenda in advance of the meeting. You can give copies of this agenda to the temporary "chairperson" or to the Staff Liaisons who will attend the meetings.

Here are some items which should appear on the agenda:
1. Discussion and tentative agreement about the general items of concern and interest to the Parent Sub-Committee. In other words, the kinds of areas and interests parents would like to discuss and investigate during the next several months. (These may change throughout the year and do not need to be "permanent.")
2. Selection of an alternate representative the Classroom Comittee.
3. Selection of a representative to the Classroom Comittee.
4. Selection of a Chairperson.

Let us give you a suggestion which could make these meetings even more productive: **Be sure that each staff liaison knows about and plans to attend the Parent Sub-Committee meetings.**

Before the Parent Sub-Committee meets, assemble all the staff who will act as liaisons and conduct a review of two things:

1. The purpose of the Parent Sub-Committee and what they can and should do; and
2. The job of the Staff Liaison. Be sure all staff are aware that they can only advise and help. They cannot vote on decisions; they cannot tell the parents how to vote; and they can have no official function.

At this point, let us turn to the questions of what the Parent Sub-Committees can and should do. We now have a good "vehicle" for parent participation. Let's look at the content.

Chapter VI
What Are Parents Interested In?

TOPICS OF DISCUSSION

Parent Involvement Coordinators often say:
What can we do to get parents interested?
What about the School and its Program will interest parents the most?

Now that you've seen a structure which could get all the parents actively involved and participating in your program, you will want some ideas about how to help the parents use their groups most effectively.

What would interest parents most? Perhaps you are a parent, but surely you have known many parents. Test your own knowledge and memory by answering the following questions.

1. If a group of parents who do not know each other gets together, they will probably discuss:
   a. their jobs
   b. their children
   c. their parents
   d. politics
   e. none of these.

2. One things all parent share in common is a concern for:
   a. whom the next President will be
   b. local community programs
   c. getting better jobs
   d. their children's welfare
   e. none of these.

3. Most parents would be interested in talking about:
   a. problems their children and other children in the class are having
   b. the school budget
   c. school staff

d. the roles of the Parent Involvement Council
   e. none of these.

4. Parents would find a discussion of the school budget:
   a. very boring
   b. not related to them
   c. very interesting.

5. Most parents would feel that the job of screening staff is the responsibility of:
   a. the Program Director
   b. the School Board
   c. the Parent Involvement Council
   d. the parents themselves.

People are unpredictable. You cannot say definitely how they will react. But the following answers are most likely to be correct for most situations: 1. b, 2. d, 3. a, 4. b, 5. a.

All these questions point to the central fact that one thing all parents in a school program have in common is their concern for their children. And if they believe their children are getting a quality experience, they are satisfied. Additionally, they may also realize that their child's entry into the program is their first step in a process that will continue for many years.

Parents are not likely to see the program as a means of educating themselves, they will see it as a place to educate their children. And most parents will participate in efforts they believe will help their children to have a better educational experience. Few parents will participate if they find that participation really means teaching parents. Yet so much of the history of parent involvement efforts has been just that: attempts on the part of school staff to teach the parents things that are often unrelated to their children.

So, to get real parent involvement, you must help your school to get out of the parent education mode and into the Parent Involvement mode.

Look at this idea more closely. The following chart should illustrate what we mean.

The following are unrelated to parent involvement:
A. Deciding whom should be hired for the classroom.
B. Making decisions about the curriculum, its development and interpretation.
C. Reading grants, interpreting budgets, and making program decisions.
D. Being asked to get involved with community affairs because they have a child in the school.

But the program has:
A. Told the parents that the hiring of staff is something in which they should participate.
B. Told parents to review the curriculum and give their reactions.
C. Given the parents instruction in how the curriculum is developed and how to interpret and follow the curriculum.
D. Told parents they should know about grants and should help make budget decisions.
E. Told parents that one of the chief benefits of the Classroom Comittee and the Parent Involvement Council is to bring about improvements in the community.

Before you say, "This isn't true, many of the parents I know are interested in those things," stop and think. Yes, some parents are interested. Those are the ones who will come to the meetings. They are the ones who will be most willing to help you. But unless your program is unusual, it has probably been very difficult to get most of the parents involved in your program. That's because they haven't been interested in these kinds of things; it's because they haven't understood that what your program has been asking them to do will help their children.

You need to get parent participation in all phases of your program that relate to the education of their children. But first you must get the parents' attention. You must get them interested. Let's look at a chart of some things that might interest parents:

Parents Do Want:
A. To learn about any special problems their children have.
B. To learn where their children are unique and different and where they are just like other children.
C. To learn special "tips" and information related to their children's welfare.
D. To be able to talk with someone if they feel their children have been mistreated.
E. To be able to discuss and do something about any special problems they may have with regard to their children such as transportation, safety, etc.
F. To follow their children's progress in the school system.

The Child Development Center Could:

A. Arrange to have teachers talk with the parents about the progress and problems of their children.
B. Arrange to have the teachers describe the behavior of the children they deal with and discuss what is normal, what is abnormal, what are "stages," etc.
C. Arrange for special lectures videos, books, etc. about toys and other items safe for children's, cognitive and social/emotional development.
D. Arrange for parents to be able to talk with other parents and staff about any concerns they have.
E. Arrange for a meaningful parent group which can put pressure on staff, or which can work out special problems in their own way.

This list isn't complete. Part of your job with parents and staff is to expand this list. In fact, you may remember that one of the items of business on the agenda for the first Parent Sub-Committee meeting is for the parents to make a list of things that really interest them.

But it will never be enough to simply ask the parents what they would like to talk about. They will need your help and imagination. The point we want to emphasize here is that to make your parent program a success, you must make parent involvement focus on the children first.

Does this mean that the school and parent groups cannot be a vehicle for community change? Absolutely not. It means that you must first organize the parents around the issue they all know they have in common and which is their first priority. After you have done this and the parents discover that they can have an influence as a group, then they will be ready to look at other things they can do. In fact you may not have to give them any help. Many parent groups will become more involved with community issues when the need arises.

In this chapter, we've seen that the school's Parent Involvement Program can focus on two broad concerns and objectives: student development and community change. You have read that a Parent Program will be most likely to get off to a successful beginning if it concentrates first on student development and later focuses on community concerns.

This is a difficult philosophy. Before we end this chapter, participate with us in an exercise which may help you to see the difference between these two objectives and will help you test how well you understand them.

Community Change and Student Development

The following statements each represent either Community Development or Student Development objectives. If you believe the statement is a Community Development objective, draw a circle around "COMMUNITY." If you believe it is a Student Development objective, draw a circle around "STUDENT."

1. The school will help parents to gain special insight and knowledge about their children's growth and behavior.
   COMMUNITY   **STUDENT**

2. The school will help the parents to form a united group so that they may better their community and family.
   COMMUNITY   **STUDENT**

3. The school will provide parents with an opportunity to approve the staff who teach their children.
   COMMUNITY   **STUDENT**

4. The school will give the parents special assistance on what they can do at home to promote the child's educational growth.
   COMMUNITY   **STUDENT**

5. The school will provide local parents with an opportunity to become employees of the School.
   COMMUNITY   **STUDENT**

6. The school will ask parents to assist in fund-raising for the program.
   COMMUNITY   **STUDENT**

7. The program will provide parents with an opportunity to discuss differences in the growth and development of their children with other parents and teachers.
   COMMUNITY   **STUDENT**

8. Parents will be able to describe the differences they have observed in their children as a result of the school.
   COMMUNITY   **STUDENT**

9. Parents will have the opportunity to discuss and seek solutions for any special problems they encounter with their children at home.
   COMMUNITY   STUDENT

10. Parents will be taught how and why lesson plans and curricula are developed.
    COMMUNITY   STUDENT

The answers are as follows: 1. STUDENT, 2. COMM, 3. COMM, 4. STUDENT, 5. COMM, 6. COMM, 7. STUDENT, 8. STUDENT, 9. STUDENT, 10. COMM.

Let's review them briefly.

1. Helping parents to gain knowledge and insights about their children is a Student Development objective. The focus is directly on helping and learning more about the child.

2. Forming the parents into a united group for any purpose is primarily a Community Change objective. It might benefit the child enormously, but it is not an effort directly concerned with the student.

3. Approving the staff who will teach the children is also primarily a Community Change activity. It gives the parents a chance to make decisions about people who will affect their lives and the lives of their children. It does not contribute directly to greater knowledge about being a parent or about the children.

4. Special assistance on what the parent can do at home to be more effective is a Student Development objective.

5. The chance to become an employee of the program is a Community Change objective. It helps the community by providing employment. Indirectly, it should also help the children and help the parents to be better parents, but the key word here is indirectly.

6. Assisting with fund-raising efforts is also a Community Change activity. It doesn't get the parents involved in the running and continuation of the program, but, as in the last statement, it helps them only indirectly with the development of their children.

7. An opportunity to compare differences in the growth of their children directly and with the staff and other parents is a Student activity.

8. For parents to be made aware of the differences they have observed in their children as a result of the School Program is a Student Development activity.

9. As in statement number eight, for parents to have an opportunity to discuss and seek solutions for special problems they are encountering with their children is directly a Student Development activity.

10. This is one of the most difficult: in our view, teaching parents about how lesson plans are formulated is not a Student Development activity. It is more a parent development activity, so we circle COMMUNITY. Our decision is based on the assumption that parents do not and will never become overly active in the development of curricula. The important point to keep in mind here is you will probably be most successful if you begin you Parent Involvement program by focusing chiefly on Student Development objectives. Then, after you have got your program firmly under way, you can begin to turn to Community Change activities.

Chapter VII
Parent Involvement And The Child Development Director

Parent Involvement Program staff often say:

"I can't get my Parent Program under way without the cooperation and support of my School Director — how do I get it?"

"My Program Director doesn't seem to really care about parent involvement. How can I find out whether that's true; and if that is true, what can I do?"

These are good questions. You can't have meaningful parent involvement without the full cooperation and support of your School Director. He or she must understand what you are doing and support it. But what about the possibility that the Program Director doesn't really care about parent involvement?

First, we believe that almost all Program Directors want parent involvement, if they can find a way to get it which doesn't disrupt their programs and require an impossible amount of their time.

Even if they want parent involvement, many Directors are probably a little afraid of it. What are some of the reasons they might be afraid of it? Think of some reasons and write your answers down here.

Did you skip that first exercise? If so, go back and spend a moment with it. It's important that you begin to get some understanding and sympathy for your Director's problems if you are going to convince him or her to help you get a strong Parent Involvement Program started.

Now let us share some of our ideas with you and why the Director could be uncertain about parent involvement. Compare your responses with ours.

1. He or she might be afraid parents would make bad policy decisions.
   Can you think of how this might happen? What about the interviewing of staff? Are parents really qualified to know what kind of person would make the best teacher?

2. The Director might be afraid he or she would lose control of the program. How could that happen? One example would be if the expenditure of budget items became a political issue in the community. For example, if a group with little knowledge of the internal needs of a program tried to get money spent for an unnecessary new bus instead of new computers.

3. The Director might be afraid he would have to spend too much time with parents of individual committees and wouldn't have enough time for the greater needs of the program.

4. The Program Director might be afraid that some of this staff would use the parent groups to resist his direction or leadership.

5. The Director might not believe that effective parent involvement is possible.

These are valid worries. As Parent Involvement Coordinator, you must help your Program Director see why these kinds of problems don't have to occur. And you will have to help to find ways to stop them from happening.

You may also have another very significant problem — convincing your Director to let you use your time in the way you think best.

Does your Director use you as a "Go-For?" Does your Director ask you to do errands and take on special projects which don't have much to do with parent involvement? In many programs, the Parent Involvement Coordinator is more like a special assistant to the Program Director. If this is your situation, you have probably become very valuable to your Director for these kinds of activities. If so, you must persuade you Director to let you take on a different role.

This is very important. You will have to persuade your Director. You will have to convince him or her that is worthwhile to let you use your time differently. You may even have to convince your Director that you are competent to decide how to use your time. Don't expect your Director to understand your job as you now understand it. It is up to you to convince the Director that your time should be spent in matters dealing exclusively with parent involvement.

So you must show your Program Director that:

1. Your Parent Program will be a good thing and will not make his or her job more difficult.
2. You have a plan for parent involvement that must have support from the Director.

3. You must be able to make your own decisions about how you spend you time and that most of your time should go into parent involvement activities.

How do you convince your Director of these things? One way is to have a plan. A good, clear, simple plan which your Director and the staff can see and understand easily. The next few pages will show you one way to present such a plan.

First, prepare a short memorandum to your Director describing the objectives of your Parent Involvement Program and the methods you propose for achieving them. The following is a sample memorandum. Use this sample to prepare a memo that is appropriate to your program.

MEMORANDUM

To: school Director
Date:
From: Parent Involvement Coordinator
Subject: The proposed Parent Involvement Program for (year)

I. Purpose of Memo

This memorandum will outline for you the proposed activities of our Parent Involvement Program for the school year ____ to ____ . It will then describe briefly the methods and approaches I propose for achieving our parent involvement objectives. Finally, it will recommend for your approval the support and activities which you and the other program staff might provide to make the Parent Involvement Program a success.

II. Objectives of the Parent Program

The Parent Program will have the following broad objectives:

1. To fulfill the guidelines for parent involvement as outlined in program regulations.

2. To provide the parents of the children in our School with a way to participate in the making of policies which will affect them and their children.

3. The provide the parents and the children in our program with a way to benefit from the skills and resources of our staff.

4. To provide the parents of the children in our program with an opportunity to learn more about each other and the needs of the community.

III. The Approach to Parent Involvement

The approach we use involves three parts.

Part 1

Orient the staff of the program with the general goals and approaches of the Parent Program and get mutual agreements as to individual staff roles and responsibilities. In brief, to bolster staff involvement and participation.

Part 2

Divide the parents into small groups within which effective participation is possible.

PART 3

Assist with the forming of a Classroom Comittee which will be representative of the parents.

IV. Recommended Action
To get our Parent Involvement Program operational as quickly as possible, I recommend that we meet soon so that I may describe the Parent Involvement plan to you in greater detail and discuss with you any suggestions or modifications you propose.

After you have given your School Director a memo explaining your goals and objectives and requesting a follow-up meeting, you will want to contact the Director and set a time to meet with him or her. Be sure to allow plenty of time for your meeting.

Prepare For Your Meeting With The Director

Let's assume that your Director has agreed to a meeting. You will want to prepare very carefully and you must have some of the work already completed.

We suggest that you make a list of the work you must complete before your meeting and another list of the things you want to accomplish in your meeting. Here are some suggestions:

To Do Before the Meeting with the Director:

1. Have a complete list of all parents' names.
2. Have tentative sub-committees established.
3. Prepare flip-charts for presentation.

Item number 3 on this list can be very important. Prepared flip-charts are much easier for two or more people to follow and they will show the Director that you have done a professional job of planning.

Creating a chart:

1. List different parent sub-committees, including staff and parents that you recommend be in them.
2. Include pictures or graphs indicating the parent involvement structure you propose. (You may want to draw a picture like the one on page 25)
3. Make a calendar of events detailing:
   a. When you propose to orient the staff.
   b. When you propose to orient the parents.
c. When the first sub-committee meetings will be held.
d. When the first Classroom Comittee meeting will be held.
e. When the first Parent Involvement Council meeting will be held.
f. List of the responsibilities of the Director and the staff for the Parent Program.

When you have completed the preparations for your meeting with the Director, take a few minutes and write down what you want to accomplish in your meeting. Your list might look like this:

To be sure the Director fully understands the proposed Parent Involvement Program.
To get the Director's approval and support of the proposed program.
To get the Director to agree on the dates for the orientation of the staff and parents.

You are now ready to meet with the Director. Expect him or her to ask a lot of questions. Expect him or her to be doubtful. After all, you are proposing something new. Expect your Director to suggest changes, too.

There are some parts of the program you are proposing which can and perhaps should be changed to meet the special needs of your particular program. Be flexible and support changes which will make the program work better for your situation. Be firm and insistent about not making changes which will harm the Parent Program. Of course, if your Director insists, you must make whatever chances he or she demands. But you can state very clearly that you feel certain changes will harm the program. In most cases, you certainly will cause your Director to think again and even change his or her mind.

How do you know what changes would help the program? How do you know which changes would hurt the program? It's not going to be easy. To get ready for your talk with the Director, practice by answering the following questions he or she might ask about the program you are suggesting. Base your choice of answer on whether you feel the change can or cannot be made without hurting the program.

Circle: (A) Yes, if you think the change could be made without hurting the program; (B) Yes, if you think the change could be made without hurting the program, but would not be desirable; (C) No, if you think the change could not be made without hurting the program.

How would you reply if the Director asks:

1. Do we have to have a separate orientation for both the staff and parents? Can't you give everyone one big orientation? **A B C**

2. Do we need all of these Sub-Committees? **A B C**

3. Can't we just have one Parent Committee groups and have it meet more often? **A B C**

4. Do we have to have a staff member assigned to each Sub-Committee? Can't you be the staff coordinator for all the Sub-Committees? **A B C**

5. Do we have to follow this strict schedule of having the Sub-Committees meet during the first ten days of the month, the Classroom Sub-Committee meeting between the eleventh and twentieth days, and the School Council meeting between the twenty-first and thirtieth days? **A B C**

6. Do we need such an extensive Parent Program? It's so much trouble, why don't we just continue as we are? **A B C**

Recommended Responses:

1. For the first question, the recommended reply is (B): 'Yes, but..." It would be possible to orient both the staff and parents together; but this is much less desirable. When you assemble all the parents together for your orientation, you will want to have a lot of help. You will want the staff to know and understand the program and so they will not appear doubtful in front of the parents.

2. The answer to this question must be (C): an absolute "NO." You must have the Sub-Committees. That is the heart of the program. No one can participate effectively in a group of fifteen, twenty, or more people. The key to success of your program will be to have your parents in small enough groups for them to speak and participate freely. Another advantage to the Sub- Committees is that they allow the parents the option of choosing when and where they want to meet. With only one group meeting at a time, there is a greater chance that many will not attend because of conflicts in their schedules or because of transportation problems.

3. You could reply (B): "Yes, but..." to this question, but it is a big but. Without the participation of the staff in each Parent Sub-Committee, you lose an important part of the program. Therefore, (A) is the recommended response. The presence of a staff member will help insure that the meetings occur and that they occur when the parents will talk about the program and its concerns. Also, the staff member provides valuable assistance in that he or she can explain curricula and policy questions. He or she can talk about the children from first-hand observation and describe particular problems any children may be having. Often, the teacher will be able to help with recommended solutions.

4. The answer to this question could be (A): "Yes." You remember that the schedule of meetings was recommended so that the Parent Sub-Committees would be able to make recommendations to the Classroom Comittee. Similarly, the Parent

Involvement Council meeting should occur each month after the Classroom Comittee has met so that it can make recommendations and suggest issues for discussion to the Parent Involvement Council. This would be a good arrangement if you could work it out, but it is not crucial to the success of the program.

5. The answer to this questions is (C) "No."

Did you answer them all correctly? If not, don't be discouraged — that's why we are practicing. If you go back and reread the approaches outlined in earlier chapters while these explanations are still fresh in your mind, you will probably find that it is all much clearer to you.

Let's return now to your meeting with your Director. If you have discussed these questions and explained your program, you are ready to ask your Director if he or she likes the approach and will support you. Be satisfied if he or she will support you, even if a few doubts remain. If you accomplish this much, you have done a lot. You're ready to continue.

Summary

This chapter reminded you that the support of your Director is absolutely essential for the success of your program. You've learned some ways to get that support by insuring that your Director is thoroughly informed of your plans and intentions and has had a chance to say yes or no. In short, we've shown you a way to get a kind of "contract" with your Director for what you will do and how you will go about doing it.

Of course, once you have won the support of your Director you can't just forget about him or her. You must keep him or her informed of your progress and activities. You must check with your Director routinely, especially if you want to meet with the staff or do something special. You want to be sure that your Director's support increases. And the best way to do that is to keep him or her continually involved in the Parent Program.

On the other hand, you will now have a contract with your Director. And if he or she forgets and asks you to do an errand or some job which takes you away from the busy job of organizing parents and overseeing the Sub-Committees and Classroom Comittee, you may gently remind him or her that you have made an agreement. In other words, if you stick to your contract, you will find that it protects you and your time, as well as the program.

Chapter VIII
Parent Involvement and the Staff

Many Parent Coordinators Say:

Staff members don't think our work is important.
We can't have parent involvement without the staff's help and they don't seem to want to help.
The staff of our program doesn't understand why it should be involved. They say parent involvement is "our job" and not theirs.

Should staff be involved in parent involvement programs? How much?
How can you get staff involved? In this chapter we will look for answers to these kinds of questions.

How To Get Staff Participation

You already know the first thing you must do to get staff participation. Can you guess what we have in mind?

That's right. The first thing you must do is get the full support of your Director as outlined in
in Chapter VII.

Your approach to the staff can be similar to what you did with the Director. The first step is to inform the staff fully about your program. You will want to be sure that each staff member knows the following things:

1. Why the school needs parent involvement, how it can help parents, how it can help staff and the school, and how it can help the children.
2. The goals of your Parent Program.
3. The structure of your Parent Program, the Parent Involvement Council, the Classroom Comittee, and the Parent Sub-Committees.
4. The amount of participation required and ways in which the staff can participate.

ORIENT THE STAFF

The best way to be sure your staff knows these facts about parent involvement is to conduct an orientation and "training session." This is a meeting which all staff attend. To do a proper orientation which gets the staff of your school really involved, you will need about two and a half days. The best time to do this is before the program begins; however, if your program has already begun, you will have to spread it out over several days or maybe even weeks. Once you have secured the cooperation of your Director, you may want to send a memo to all the staff, outlining your objectives. A sample follows:

MEMORANDUM

Date:
TO: Director, Central Staff, Teachers and Aides
FROM: Parent Coordinator
RE: Staff Workshops, Preparing for Parent Involvement
Time:
Day and Date:
Place:

The workshops have the following objectives:

1. To help the staff look at ways that parent involvement can be used to make the program more effective.

2. To help the staff outline a program for opening day in each class with the parents of that class.

3. To help staff prepare a plan for home visiting to inform and promote parents' attendance at program openings.

4. To help the staff learn techniques for involving parents and keeping them involved.

5. To help the staff develop the skills they need to implement the opening day program.

The approach to the beginning of this school will be different than in previous years. We are requiring that parents accompany their children on the first day of the program. The staff will assist parents with the opening-day programs which we will prepare at the staff workshops.

Please come prepared to participate in this new approach to parent involvement.

We will spend two weeks preparing for and implementing the new plan. The first few days will be spent on objectives one, two and three, with home visits to be made on the remaining three days. The first day of the second week will be spent on objectives four and five before the program ends for the year.

Your cooperation, participation and enthusiasm are greatly appreciated.

An Overview of the Staff Orientation

The complete staff orientation program should take place over a period of two weeks. The following calendar will give you an idea of what happens each day. (The example is based upon a model with three schools. Modify it according to your particular situation.)

	MONDAY	TUESDAY	WEDNESDAY	THURSDAY	FRIDAY
WEEK ONE	Orientation for the Directors and staff of all Centers	Orentation for the Directors and staff of all Centers	Staff make home visits	Staff make home visits	Staff make home visits
WEEK TWO	Directors and staff meet tomake final preparations for opening day	Day off if all work is completed	Center 1 Opens	Center 2 Opens	Center 3 Opens

As you can see from this calendar, all the staff must be orienting the parents with the Parent Involvement Program. Here is the meaning of the Calendar in more detail:

Week One:
Days one and two (Monday and Tuesday):

During these two days, you will help to insure that the staff understand the Parent Involvement Program and their role in it. Finally, they will plan the home visits to prepare for opening day when all the parents and children will come to the class. Most importantly, these two days will help you gain their cooperation and support.

Days three, four and five (Wednesday, Thursday and Friday):
During these three days each staff member will visit the homes of the parents. By this time, you will know which staff are working with which Parent Sub-Committees. You will want to be sure that the staff member visits the parent who will make up the Sub-Committee to which he or she will be an advisor.

Week Two:
Day One (Monday):
All the staff will reassemble to compare their experiences from their home visits. They will then complete their final design for the opening day.

Day Two (Tuesday):
If all the work and all the preparations for the opening day have been completed, the staff will have this day off to rest.

Days Three, Four and Five (Wednesday, Thursday and Friday):
During these days, each program will have its "opening day" orientation for parents and children.

Note Carefully: This plan requires that staff of each classroom help each other. For example, if your program has three classrooms, each would open on a different day. The day each School opens, the staff from the other programs will take care of the children. That will leave the staff of the opening classroom free to get to know the parents.

Now let's look at the first two days of orientation:

ORIENTATION

Days One and Two: Staff Orientation

These are some of the most important days of your program year. If they go well, you'll have the staff with you and supporting the Parent Involvement Program. Here is a "design" for what to do during these days. It has been used in several schools with considerable success.
The "design" is based upon the idea that adults learn best when they are involved in their own learning. Workshops create an environment which encourages this participation and involvement. Try this little exercise to learn from some of your experiences.

Think about workshops and meetings you have attended. List some of the things you liked and disliked about them.

Of the things you liked, think about what you might do to include them in your dealings with the Parent Involvement Program.
Of the things you disliked, what could have been done to make them more productive and enjoyable?

Read through this design carefully to be sure that you understand it. After you are sure you understand the design, you may find some areas you would like to change to make them more suitable for your program.

Staff Orientation To the Parent Involvement Program

Exercise I

Day: Day 1
Time: 9:00 a.m. (first session, one hour)
Purpose: To inform the staff about what will happen during the two days and of the general objectives of the Parent Involvement Program.
Exercise: Lecture
Responsible Party: Lecturer, Program Director or Parent Involvement Coordinator
Group Configuration: All staff assembled together
Materials/Resources Needed: Prepared flip charts, view graphs and overhead projectors, if available.

A Word about Doing Workshops:

It is important that you take a few minutes before beginning each session to loosen up the group with whom you are working. You should try to "set a climate" where both school staff and parents will be comfortable and happy to be there. A game, a song, a joke, etc. that brings laughter may be all that is needed to create an atmosphere in which you can begin to accomplish your objectives.

Sample Lecture:

Welcome. It's a pleasure to see you all here together again as we get ready for another successful year. During the next thirty or forty minutes, I would like to outline why we have set aside these two days and what we expect to achieve.

We hope to use these next two days for several purposes. First and foremost, we want to develop together a strategy which will help to get parents really involved in their children's education. We have some ideas and approaches which we would like to share with you. As you know, meaningful parent involvement means interaction with the total staff of the program. This means we will need your full cooperation, support and participation in parent involvement this year. We hope to begin that involvement on opening day, and so a second result of these two days will be an opening day program which we have all designed together and in which we all participate.

Before we discuss that further, however, let me review some of the reasons why we have parent involvement and some of the objectives of our Parent Involvement Program. Why do we have parent involvement? Is it really necessary?

(At this point the speaker should stop and give members of the group an opportunity to suggest some answers to these questions. Take approximately five minutes to hear from a few members before proceeding.)

As some of you said, perhaps the most important reason for parent involvement is that if it occurs properly, the parents will be able to support the growth of their children at home and to help insure that their children get a quality educational experience. Here is a summary of some of the reasons we know of for having a strong Parent Involvement Program in our school.

(Have a flip chart prepared with these points on it or if necessary, list these on a flip chart as you talk.)

1. We must have a strong Parent Involvement Program in which all the parents have an opportunity to be involved in many educational aspects of the program.

2. A good Parent Involvement program can strengthen the program by giving parents a chance to support the curricula of the classroom in their homes.

3. A Parent Involvement Program can assist the staff in learning the special problems and needs of the children in their classrooms.

Here are the objectives that we have for today that hopefully will be helpful to us in planning the Parent Involvement Program:

(Have a flip chart prepared with these points on it, entitled Objectives for Today:)

* A different way to look at each child's home
* Deciding what we need to know from parents
* Developing techniques for getting information

There isn't going to be much more lecturing for the rest of these sessions. We're going to do some work in small groups as well as some exercises which should help us get to our objectives. We hope that what is planned will be interactive, fun, informal, and that it will incorporate all our combined resources. With this overview, I suggest that we begin our first session.

Exercise Two:

Day: Day 1
Time: 10:00 a.m. (second session, two hours)
Purpose: To help the staff begin thinking about the needs of the children and the kinds of homes and environments in which they live.
Exercises: Small Group Exercises, Large Group Discussion
Responsible Party: Parent Involvement Coordinator gives instructions to the groups and helps with the reporting of the results.
Group Configuration: Participants are divided into groups of five and six for the first hour. For the second hour, all are assembled together. If more than one school is involved, have the groups composed of representatives from each school.
Materials/Resources Needed: Flip charts or large newsprint for each small group (six or eight pads). Boxes of crayons containing several colors for each group. Enough space or meeting rooms for each group to work separately.

SAMPLE LECTURE:

(The leader will ask the participants to divide into groups of no more than six participants. Be sure that each group has a flip chart and a room or enough space where it can work apart from the others without distraction.)

For this exercise, we would like you to divide yourselves into small groups. No group should have more than six members. The assignment is for each group to draw a picture which it feels shows what the home of your class's average child is like. Use your imagination. Show what you feel is important.

You will have approximately one hour for this exercise. We will then reassemble and compare and discuss our drawings. Each group may want to select a spokesperson to explain its drawing.

(After thirty to forty minutes have elapsed, you may want to check with each group to see if it is nearly complete. If all finish sooner than one hour, reconvene the group. After one hour encourage those who are not yet finished to do so and reconvene the group as quickly as possible. You can then introduce the second part of this exercise.)

Let's now share the results of this past hour's exercise. Could someone show his or her group's drawing and explain it to us?

(Allow each group sufficient time to present its picture.)

The leader may want to ask the following kinds of questions:
1. Has your group seen homes which are really like this?
2. What are some of the possible effects on a child of living in a home like this?
3. Does the home situation have any relevance to our program?
4. Do we know that the home is like this or do we hope it is?
5. How does it compare with your home?

Exercise Three:

Day: Day 2
Time: 9:00 a.m. (first session, three hours)
Purpose: To inform the staff of the Parent Involvement structure and the way "opening day" can be used to begin the Parent Involvement Program; to cause the staff to begin thinking about ways parents can feel needed by the program and can feel helped as well.
Exercise: Lecture, Small and Large Group Exercises, Questions and Answer Period
Responsible Party: Parent Involvement Coordinator
Group Configuration: All participants from all programs are assembled together and then divide into small groups of five or six persons. Then the small groups will reassemble into one large group.
Materials/Resources Needed: Flip chart, paper, pens

The leader will want to present a brief lecture on the new Parent Involvement structure. The following lecture is offered as a sample of what might be said. Be sure to modify and adapt it to conform to what actually occurred on Day One and to the needs of your group.

SAMPLE LECTURE:

Today we looked at our ideas about what the average child's home is like. We saw that the typical child may have a lot of needs which the program might help with. In addition, some of us began to see some ways our program could benefit from a chance to talk with parents and learn about individual children's needs.

This afternoon, we will explore that possibility further. We will see what kinds of information and help we think we might like to get from the parents and then spend a little time brainstorming about how we might get that information.

To do this I would like you to return to the small groups you were in this morning and do the following assignment:

(Have this assignment written on a flip chart so the leader may write it out as he or she talks.)

In small groups, make a list of all the items or subjects you as staff might find out from parents about the children in your classrooms which could help you provide a richer experience for them. Some examples of questions you might ask are:
Does he talk to people?
Can he dress himself?
Does he look at books? What are his favorite foods?
Is he allergic to anything?
Does he have temper tantrums?

You will have approximately one and half hours to complete this exercise.

(After one and a half hours, reassemble to a large group and ask each small group to report. You might say:)

Let's see what each group came up with. It will be interesting to see what the differences are, if any. We will want to keep all of the questions that were generated by this exercise because they will become the basis for work to be done by the sub-committees in the coming year.

(Let each group present its list and offer any explanations it wishes to make about any items. You might have the spokesperson from each group take turns, each presenting a separate item from his or her list.)

The leader might want to ask the following kinds of questions:
1. Would knowing the answers to the questions we have listed here be helpful to you in doing your job?
2. Are you seeing Parent Involvement any differently than before?
3. Can you think of some ways in which we might get the answers to some of the items we have listed?

(After each group has presented its list, the leader will want to introduce the final exercise of the afternoon. He or she might do so in the following way:)

Now that we have an idea of the kind of information and input we would like from parents, we need to develop some strategies for ways to get that information. For this next exercise, however, let's try to have some fun as well. The assignment is to return to your small groups and develop a skit, a little play, or even some role play situations showing how you might get some information you need.

(If there is confusion about the meaning of this assignment, you might give the group the following example. If one group decided that a home visit could get the necessary information, that group might develop a role play between a staff member and an imaginary mother showing what questions would be asked and how they might be asked.)

You will have approximately one hour for this assignment and then we will reassemble and hear each group's presentations.

(After one hour, reassemble the group and have each small group give its presentation. After all the presentations, close the day's exercises with some remarks like the following:)

Today we have looked at some of the ways parents could help us to develop a stronger, more relevant program for our students. I think we have seen that if we can get parents involved and working with us, we can achieve a lot together.

We will spend tomorrow developing our plans for parent involvement for the next year. One of the most important features of this plan is our orientation of the parents on opening day; and tomorrow we will spend much of our time planning for that orientation. Since the orientation cannot be successful with out the parents being there, it will be important for us to plan for the home visits we will be making for the remainder of the week during which we will let the parents know the details of when and where to come and what to expect when they get there.

Exercise Four:

Day: Day Two
Time: 9:00 a.m. (first session, three hours)
Purpose: To inform the staff of the Parent Involvement structure and the way "opening day" can be used to begin the Parent Involvement Program; to cause the staff to begin thinking about how parents can feel needed by the program and can feel helped as well.
Exercise: Lecture, Small and Large Group Exercises, Question and Answer Panel
Responsible Party: Parent Involvement Coordinator
Group Configuration: All participants from all Centers are assembled together and then divided into small groups of five or six persons. Then the small groups will reassemble into one large group.

SAMPLE LECTURE:

Yesterday was a long day, but we accomplished a great deal. We talked about the typical home of the child and what some of his needs might be. We then looked at how the Child Development Center could help the child meet some of these needs. We talked about how it would be helpful if we worked closely with the parents, sharing information which would help us do a better job. Finally, we spent the last hours developing strategies for ways we could get information from the parents.

One fact is clear. If we can make parent involvement work, we can create a better experience for our children. We can do a service for the parents and, in the long run, we can do something to help improve the communities we serve.

Another fact is clear. No one can make parent involvement happen individually. If we leave parent involvement to be done by the Parent Coordinator or the Director or by someone else, we will have only token involvement. This is because parent involvement involves all of us. After all, who are the parents to be involved with? They are to be involved with all the staff.

As you know, we have been talking about parent involvement in schools for a long time. Many of you have worked hard in past years to get parents involved. But we haven't had the success we've wanted. So, this year we're going to try something different. We're going to offer and recommend to the parents an organizational structure which should make it easier for each individual parent to be a part of the decisions, policies and programs of the school. This structure should also help the parents to use more fully the resources of the school to improve their abilities as parents and perhaps even their communities.

Let me explain this structure in a little more detail. You all know that the primary vehicle for parent involvement is the Classroom Comittee. All parents are supposed to be on that committee. All parents are supposed to make recommendations and to review and approve various aspects of our program from that committee. They elect representatives to the Parent Involvement Council from the Classroom Comittee.

The Classroom Comittee will continue to be the central voice of parents. But, to make it more useful, we suggest that the parents form Sub-Committees, either composed of parents with children in the same classroom or of parents who live in the same geographical area, whichever is most feasible.

If the parents accept this idea, these Sub-Committees will meet monthly at a time and place of the committees' choosing. Each Sub-Committee will have representatives who will attend monthly Class meetings. Of course, any and all parents would be able and welcome to attend. But these representatives would pledge themselves to attend.

Why take this approach? First, after careful study, it is clear that there are too many parents to accomplish much in one large monthly meeting. People talk and think best in small groups with people they know.

Secondly, with only one meeting occurring each month, there is a greater chance that more people will not be able to attend because of conflicts in schedule or transportation problems. By having smaller groups meet in places of their own choosing at time of their convenience, it is likely that more parents will get together more often.

So, to repeat the proposed plan quickly, we are going to try to help set up a parent involvement structure which will look like this:

(Have the following diagram prepared on a flip chart:)

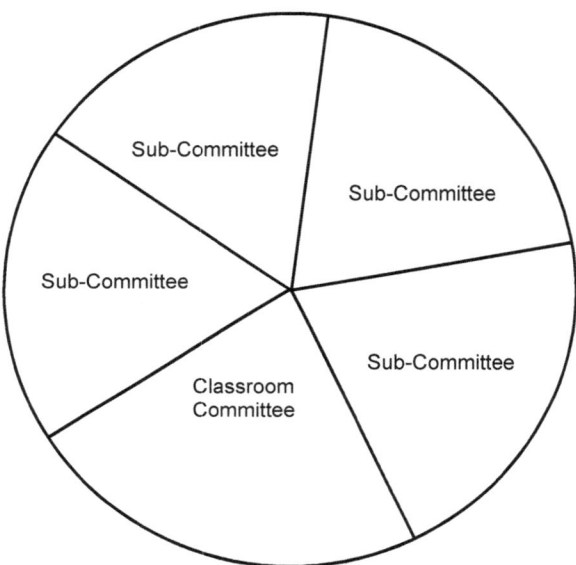

Parent Involvement Council

For this plan to be as effective as possible, there is one more important feature to it. Each staff member of the program will serve as advisor or liaison for a Sub-Committee in the program.

This will be a very important and difficult role. Each staff member will be associated with a Parent Sub-Committee, but he can only be an advisor or helper at the parents' request. He cannot vote and he should not try to influence the parents in any way. He is there to help, to clarify, and to answer questions, and to bring the school to the parents.

You could ask, "Why bother to have each of us select a Sub-Committee or be assigned to a Sub-Committee? Why not wait until the parents invite us?"

Let me try to answer that. We believe that we must do more than just sit back and wait for the parents to ask us. We don't think that's fair. We want to go out of our way to make ourselves available. We know it's not easy to ask for help. After all, the parents are meeting because we've asked them to. We've told them that this is one of the conditions of having a child in the program. So it's up to all of us to help make them make their meetings as productive as possible.

We know that you have many questions about what has been said and we know that it is important to have those questions answered if we are going to have an effective program. We realize that success depends upon you and your understanding of what has been said.

At this point, before we divide into groups with others from our center, take a few minutes to write down any questions you have about anything that has been said.

(Allow five minutes for participants to write questions. The leader will ask the participants to form groups containing all the staff members of particular schools. There should be as many groups as there are schools in the program. If possible, the maximum number for an effective group is twelve participants. Now get with the other staff that work in your school and write a list of questions that must be answered before you could carry out this new idea.)

You will have forty-five minutes to complete your list of questions. Select a spokesperson to share the questions later on.

(After thirty to forty minutes have elapsed, you may want to check with each group to see if it is nearly complete. After another ten to fifteen minutes, reconvene the large group. You can then introduce the second part of this exercise as follows:)

We are going to form a panel composed of myself, the director, the education director and other key staff that have been helping formulate plans for the new structure. We are asking that the spokesperson from the groups take turns in asking the questions developed. Our panel will attempt to answer the questions which will hopefully clarify you understanding of the intended program.

(Allow the question and answer period to continue until all are satisfied, trying not to have the period last longer than one hour. This exercise should be completed before lunch.)

Exercise Five

Day: Day 2
Time: 1:30 p.m. (second session, three hours)
Purpose: To develop a plan for making home visits.
Exercises: Chart Presentations, Small Groups, Large Group, Role Plays
Responsible Party: Parent Involvement Coordinator
Materials/Resources Needed: Flip Charts, marking pencils

The leader will want to present a brief lecture presenting a chart that has been prepared in conjunction with the Education Director. (Perhaps the chart could be presented by the Education Director.) The chart should list program openings and dates, and support staff assigned to children.

SAMPLE LECTURE:

This morning our question and answer period was very stimulating. We hope that this program is very clear in our minds and that we are now able to take part in its implementation.

The chart pictures what will occur next week in accordance with our center openings. It also shows staff assignments for each day. Remember, on the day a child development center opens, the staff of that center will be with the parents of that center and the staff of another will care for the children. Remember also that after opening day at a center, it will close for the remainder of the week, giving all centers a chance to have their opening day program.

Now look at the chart and write down where you will be on which day and what you will be doing.

Example: Week Two - Staff of Center A

Monday: Final Planning Workshop
Tuesday: With the Children of Center C at Center C
Wednesday: With the parents of my Center
Thursday: Off
Friday: With the children of Center B

(Leader will want to give about ten minutes for staff to fill out calendars and to answer questions.)

If everyone knows his or her schedule for next week, we can now get into the very important task of planning for the home visits that we will make to ask the parents to come to the opening day programs. To satisfy the questions that parents might have about the importance of opening day, we have to be sure to provide them with the necessary information. Let us return now to our center groups. Here is the assignment:

In small groups of staff from each center, develop two lists of items to be accomplished during your home visit:
1. things you want to learn about the home and the child, and
2. things you feel the parents should know about opening day at the Center.

(After the groups return, have one or two groups present their lists. If there are more than two groups, you do not need to have each one describe its list. Instead, after two groups have presented theirs, ask if there are any significant differences or additions other groups came up with.)

Now that we have a picture of what to do on our home visits, we need to talk a little more about what will happen on opening day so that we can give parents an idea about what to expect.

We are not actually going to plan the opening day program today because that part is reserved for our workshop next Monday. The list of objectives that you see here includes the things we want to accomplish on opening day so we can tell parents that this is what they can expect. We will work out the details about how to accomplish these objectives at our next workshops.

(Leader should present the following lists of objectives for opening day and ask the staff to incorporate the information into the lists that were made in the previous exercise. Be sure to adapt the objectives to your particular program.)

OBJECTIVES FOR OPENING DAY AT EACH CENTER

I. Get acquainted
   a. Staff and Parents
   b. Parents and other parents

II. Experience the Center
   a. Know the composition of the classrooms
   b. Know how the classrooms are staffed
   c. Know the rest of the staff and their jobs

III. Know the components of the school
   a. The Education Component
   b. The Nutrition Component
   c. The Social Services Component
   d. The Health Component
   e. The Parent Involvement Component
   f. Other components of your program

IV. Understand the meaning and structure of parent involvement
   a. Sub-Committees by classroom or geographic area
   b. Center committee elected by Sub-Committee
   c. Parent Involvement Council representatives elected by Center Committees

Now that you have all of the information for your home visits this week, go back to your groups and prepare a skit or role play demonstrating the visits you will be making. You will have approximately forty-five minutes, then we will reassemble and hear each group presentation.

(After forty-five minutes, reassemble the groups and have each group give its presentation. Introduce the presentation with remarks like the following:)

We will now have each group present its skit. Let us put ourselves in the role of a parent and ask ourselves this question: "Would I attend the opening day program based upon this home visit?"

(When each group finishes, hold a short discussion and ask for comments relating to that question. At the end of the presentation, close the day by saying something like the following:)

In these two days, we have worked very hard in looking at parent involvement and how it can benefit the program and how we can encourage it. Now it's time to visit parents and start to build the close relationship required to make our effort successful. Good luck on your home visits.

During Wednesday, Thursday and Friday of this orientation week, the staff will be making home visits. The Parent Involvement Coordinator and the Director as well as any other staff who may not be making home visits should be available in case any complications arise. For example, if one of the staff has a conflict and cannot make his or her scheduled visits, the Parent Involvement Coordinator or other unassigned staff member should step in and make the visit. Try to see that all parents are visited.

The following Monday, all staff from each child development center should reassemble to complete the preparations for the opening day of each of the centers. We have included a "design" for how this day might be conducted.

Exercise Six

Day: Day six
Time: 10:00 a.m. (first session, one hour)
Purpose: To help the staff make final preparations for "opening day" at the Child Development Centers
Techniques: Small Groups, Large Groups
Responsible Party: Program Director or Parent Involvement Coordinator gives the instructions to the groups and helps with the reporting out of the results.
Group Configuration: Participants are divided in to groups by Center staff for the first hour. For the next half hour, all are assembled in the total group.
For the next hour and a half, the Center staff are once again in separate groups and an additional group is formed containing the central staff.
Materials/Resources Needed: Flip charts or large newsprint for each small group, felt tip markers and masking tape.

Sample Lecture:

Good morning! Welcome back after three very busy days of home visiting. I know we all have a lot to tell about that experience and all of the information is important to us, especially as we plan for opening days at the Centers.

We think that our planning for Opening Day will be helped if we know some of the things about the people we are planning for, the parents. To do this, let us return to the center groups and complete the following assignment:

(Have this assignment written on a flip chart or the leader may write it out as he talks.) In your group, share your experiences of home visiting with one another and then list all of the things you know about the parents that will be helpful in planning an Opening Day Program. Examples of things to list are: number of parents that are coming; are they shy; are they cooperative; are they new to the school, etc. You will have approximately one hour to complete this exercise.

(After forty-five minutes, rotate among the groups to be sure they have a good ideal of who it is they will be planning Opening Day programs for. You may offer additional comments as necessary. When you are satisfied that each group's list is sufficient, call the entire group together and give the following brief lecture:

Last week, before you went on your home visits, we put up a list of objectives to accomplish on opening day.

(You may once again wish to use the flip chart you developed for these objectives.)

It will be our job today to accomplish these objectives by preparing methods using the information that we have just listed about the parents. Let's look at each of the objectives while I describe some possible ways to accomplish them. We will vary our methods to keep it interesting. (Try to avoid "lecturing" and boring repetition.)

1. *Get acquainted*
   Each of the staff members could be responsible for getting together the eight or ten parents of the Sub-Committee he or she will be working with. He could introduce himself and tell something about himself and then have each of the parents do likewise. Blank sheets of paper could be passed out with instructions for each person to draw a picture of himself and write a one-word description of his or her mood. Pictures are then passed to the right until each is returned to its owner. Some songs which are used to help children learn names can be sung in the groups.

2. *Experience the Center*
   Sub-Committee groups could take a walk through the classrooms while the staff liaison describes each of the areas.
   Parents could act as if they are children and could participate in some of the activities led by staff. The staff of the program could rotate to each group, introduce themselves, and describe some of their duties. The parents could ask questions and hold a discussion on what was said for ten minutes after each staff member speaks.

3. *Know the Components of the school*

This is primarily the job of the central staff members and our task after this lecture will help them develop some ways to do this.

4. Understand the Meaning and Structure of Parent Involvement
This is one of the most crucial parts of our Opening Day Program.

We are attempting to create three kinds of groups:
1. *The Sub-Committee*: composed of half the parents of a classroom or eight to ten parents that live close to one another.
2. *The Classroom Committee*: composed of members elected by each Sub-Committee.
3. *The Parent Involvement Council*: composed of those members elected by the Center Committee of each center for the entire program.

(The leader at this point may wish to present some of the ideas from Chapter IV that would suggest ways to accomplish this objective.)

For the purpose of planning for opening day, we are going to ask you once again to form into groups according to center. Additionally, we are going to ask the central staff (the component heads) to form a group. Here is the assignment for the center groups:

Take each of the objectives that we have just talked about and decide on a way to accomplish each for the parents that are coming to your Center on Opening Day. You will have approximately one to one and a half hours to complete this task.

(The leader may have to provide any logistical information that the groups might need, i.e. beginning and ending times of Opening Day Program, whether lunch will be served, etc. While the Classroom groups are working on that task, the central staff groups should form. You may introduce their tasks in the following way:)

As component heads, we are concerned that our departments are as well understood as possible. This would be helped if we could get a good start on opening day. For the first task, please write down individually all of the things that you do in your job. Take about fifteen minutes to do this.

(After fifteen minutes, ask if all are finished. If so, ask them to share their lists with one another.)

Would you now take turns reading your lists to the rest of the group to make sure that we all get a good idea of the things you do.

(After each person shares his or her list, ask for any comments or questions. Introduce the next task in the following way:)

Take each of your lists and identify those things on the list that depend in some way on parent involvement. Take about ten minutes to do this.

(After ten minutes, have the staff share the checked items once again. After sharing lists, give the following task:)

Of the items you have checked that could be improved by parent involvement, identify those things which should be presented to parents on opening day at the centers. When you have identified those things, prepare a number of ways that you might use to share the information with the parents on opening day. You may take the rest of the morning to come up with methods to use while the staff of the centers are deciding on methods to use to accomplish the other opening day objectives. This afternoon, you should rotate among the center groups and arrange the ways you will make your presentations at center openings.

Exercise Seven

Day: Day 6
Time: 1:00 p.m.
Purpose: To prepare activities for opening day at the Centers and set a schedule and assignments for the planned activities.
Methods: Brief lecture, Small groups.
Responsible Party: Program Director/Parent Involvement Coordinator.
Group Configuration: Participants from all centers assembled together, center groups and central staff groups.
Materials/Resources Needed: Flip chart with time/activity sheet drawn and/or individual time/activity hand-outs.

SAMPLE LECTURE:

Good afternoon. This morning we spent our time deciding how to make opening day an active experience for us and the parents. This afternoon we would like to put the finishing touches on those activities and assign them to different staff members.

(At this point, you may want to show a chart with the time/activity format drawn on it, or some other format that you feel will be useful.)

SAMPLE TIME/ACTIVITY SHEET:

Time: 9:00 a.m.
Activity: Assembly/get acquainted
Method: Song, "The more we get together;" Picture: Draw yourself and describe how you feel in one word, pass pictures around
Parties Responsible: Music Teacher, Head Teacher
Materials Needed: Pencils and paper

(Describe the Time/Activity sheet in the following way:)

Once you have decided on the things you want to do, make sure that you have a plan for how they will get done. By placing the Time, Activity, Method and People & Materials on this sheet, you can make sure that everyone will know what to do and who will be doing which activities. Be sure to leave some time for the central staff to fit their parts into your plan.

(Ask for any questions. When ready, ask the center groups and central staff to reassemble and give the following task:)

In your groups, draw a time/activity chart on large paper and fill it in with the activities you have planned. You may wish to copy your center's plan for your own use on separate sheets. The central staff should take their plan to each center group and fill in their parts. You may have as long as you need to complete this.

(You may want to rotate from group to group lending assistance. Remember, the best plan in the world is still reliant on the people who carry it out. As groups finish, you may, if time permits, have them share some of the planned activities. Some may be helpful to use in all the centers and sharing should be encouraged. This activity should take most of the afternoon. When completed, the staff should spend the remaining time planning for the children they will be working with when they are assisting in another center that is opening.)

Chapter IX
The Parent Involvement Council and the Board of Directors

This manual has shown you some ways to increase parent involvement in your schools. You've seen ways to give parents a broader, more meaningful voice in the program's affairs.

Parents will get a louder voice through a stronger Center Committee. Stronger Center Committees will mean stronger Parent Involvement Councils. How much more effective your Parent Involvement Council will be depends on at least one thing: the Council's relationship with the Board of Directors of your sponsoring institution (for example: Board of Education or Child Development Association.)

You know this is true and you know why. In most agencies, the Board of Directors has the final say. It is particularly important for policy groups to develop by-laws indicating their functions to the board of the sponsoring agency for approval. Once this occurs, the policy group becomes a legally recognized and properly structured body. A guide to assist Parent Involvement Councils in developing their own by-laws within the framework of a Community Agency appears in Appendix B. In the school, the Board of Directors and Parent Involvement Council both have policy-making responsibilities. They are both intricately involved in the policy-making process. For example, the Board of Directors wants the final say about spending funds and hiring and firing staff. Yet guidelines for most schools say the Parent Involvement Council must also be closely involved in these matters.

In your agency, what are some of the conflicts that occur as a result of this collaborative system?

Let us look again at some of the responsibilities an executive board of a sponsoring agency and its policy advisory council have according to federal guidelines.

Parent Involvement Council:

1. Recommends goals of Child Development Center.
2. Assists the Board in choosing a Program Director.
3. Recommends staff for the Child Development Center
4. Approve/Disapprove any unusual expense or use of funds.

Executive Board (of sponsoring agency):

1. Assists in choosing staff, including delegate Agency Directors.
2. Assists in choosing all professional staff.
3. Approve/Disapprove of any unusual expense or use of funds.

They look like almost identical, don't they? That's part of the problem. Both groups are similar and sometimes each feels responsible for the same things. What happens when they disagree? Usually, the Parent Involvement Council or Advisory Groups loses.

What happens to your Parent Involvement Program if the Council loses? The parents will get discouraged! They will say things like:
"Parent involvement doesn't mean anything."
"When it comes to important matters, parents don't count too much."
"They'll let the parents have a voice in the day-to-day business; but for important things, such as money and hiring, our voice doesn't count."

We've all heard these kinds of statements. You're reading this manual so that you can do something about these feelings of discouragement that parents will occasionally express.
This is one reason why you must be concerned about how the Parent Involvement Council gets along with the Board of Directors. If these groups don't get along, your program will suffer.

Whose job is it to help the Parent Involvement Council? You may be thinking that this isn't your job. You're probably right, unless your Director has specifically delegated this responsibility you. It is the Director's job. But this is a place where you can help him or her and benefit your program, as well. Here's how:

Make an appointment to go and talk with your Director about the Parent Involvement Council. Tell him or her that you want to discuss the following points:

1. Present relationships between the Board and the Parent Involvement Council, particularly any problem areas.
2. Ways to strengthen the relationship between the two groups.

If you like memos, maybe you'll want to send on like this:

Date:
To: School Director
From: Parent Involvement Coordinator
Subject: Our Parent Involvement Council and the Board

As you know, for our Parent Involvement Program to be meaningful, parents must believe that they have a real voice in the program's affairs. This means that we must have a strong and effective Parent Involvement Council.

I would like to meet with you on January 4 at 4:30 p.m. to do two things:
1. Discuss your assessment of the Parent Involvement Council's present relationship with the Board of Directors; and
2. Go over some ways we can help the Council become stronger.

Before this meeting, do some homework. Find out the names of everyone on the Parent Involvement Council and on the Board. Get answers to a number of questions, such as:

1. Is there anyone who is on both the Parent Involvement Council and the Board of Directors?
2. How many are in each group? What is the total number?
3. How often does the Board meet? The Council? (Your Council should be meeting once a month during the final 1/3 of the month.)
4. What special committees and sub-committees has the Board established?
5. What problems have the two boards had with each other? Have there been any strong clashes or disagreements?

When you meet with your Director, ask about his or her ideas concerning the two groups. Share your answers to the above questions. You need to establish agreement that: the two groups do need to work cooperatively and collaboratively; that they could probably use some help accomplishing this; and that you need to get both groups together for a training session which will help both groups work together more cooperatively. For example, some centers have found it very useful to start a session late Saturday afternoon and continue it, with breaks for meals and sleep, until late Sunday afternoon.

This is an important point. Don't let it slip by! One of your objectives with the Director is to get him or her to agree to set up a day session for both the Board of Directors and the Parent Involvement Council. You and your Director are going to use that time to "train" these two groups to work more closely and collaboratively together.

In the remainder of this chapter, we will show you several possible ways to help these two groups work more closely together. Of course you should substitute your own if you have an approach you believe is more appropriate for your situation. The important point of this chapter is that the only way to get the Board and the Parent Involvement Council to work better with one another is to actually get them working together. In other words, you must find some way to set up a joint training session.

In the next few pages, you will find a detailed design for what to do with the Parent Involvement Council and the Board when they get together. It's not very hard to follow. If you can hire a consultant or a trainer to help you, that's great! But if you don't have the money for such help, you can do it yourself. Here's how:

Let's begin by assuming your Director has said, "OK, I'll arrange for the Parent Involvement Council and the Board to meet." He or she then makes arrangements for when and where the two groups will meet. They will then follow this schedule:

Day one:

4:00 p.m. - 6:00 Meet
6:00 p.m. - 7:00 Dinner
7:00 p.m. - 9:00 Meet

Day two:

9:00 a.m.- 12:30 p.m. Meet
12:30 p.m. - 1:30 Lunch
1:30 p.m.- 5:00 Meet

This session will be similar to the session for staff and parent orientation. Everyone participates. The leader's style is relaxed and informal. You are not an "expert" or a "teacher," but a group facilitator. The following design is not as detailed as the one for staff and parent orientation. It provides you with a description of what you should say or do and ways to do it. You must plan your exact words yourself. To get comfortable with the overall design, first look over the following schedule. Then go over what happens each day in fine detail.

PARENT COUNCIL AND BOARD WORKSHOP

Day one
Time: 4:00 p.m.
Objective: Get Acquainted
Methodology: The participants may seat themselves in any way they like, usually they will sit in rows (theater style). Welcome them. Thank them for coming. Let them know that you realize it's difficult to sacrifice two days.

Point to a flip chart on which you have prepared the objectives for the session. Read it to the group. Tell the group that these are the objectives that you hope to accomplish but that if the group wants to alter or add to them, you are prepared to do so. Next, give the group some idea of the type of session it will be, what kinds of exercises you will use, and the general mood you expect to achieve. Tell them it will be hard work but interactive, fun and informal.

Pass out individual sheets of paper (8 1/2 x 11) and ask each participant to draw a picture of him or herself and write a one-word description of his or her present mood. You might do this yourself. Next, ask each person to pass his to the right and keep passing them until he receives his back again. This exercise is meant to relax the group.

Finally, each participant should be given a name tag when he or she registers. The tags are two different colors, one for the Board and one for the Parent Involvement Council. Ask the group to divide itself into small groups of six with an equal number of Board and Council representatives in each. (They can tell by the different colors of the name tags.)

The first task of the group is for individuals to introduce themselves and share their thoughts and reactions to the success of the school.

Day Two
Time: 4:30 p.m. - 6:00 p.m.

Objective: Groups Learn About Each Other

Methodology: Ask the participants to form two groups: one group of Policy Council members, the other for Board members. Give each group a sheet of large newsprint divided into two columns. Each column has a heading under which participants should list two responses:

    How We See The Other Group
    How We Think The Other Group Sees Us

Give the groups sufficient time to record their responses, then ask each group to select a representative to read and explain the responses to the entire group. The mediator can help the two groups compare answers and discuss their reactions to one another's charts.

Summarize and end this session by reminding the participants of the purpose of the workshop. It is to deal with Child Development issues. Point out that there are program guidelines that they can refer to which will help them solve particular problems. Finally, ask the participants if they need more information about the guidelines.

Time 7:00 - 9:00 p.m.

After dinner, remind the participants that they wanted to learn more about guidelines. Pass out the Guideline Questionnaire about "Parent Involvement Guidelines" to be answered by each participant. Be sure that everyone knows that these are for their own information and will not be collected.

After each participant has completed his or her questionnaire but before you give the answers, have everyone form back into groups of six with representatives from each Board. Ask the small groups to develop a "group answer sheet." Explain that if the groups use the resources of each member, they can increase the number of correct answers over the average individual score.

After all the groups are finished, read them the answers. If you have time, you might find it fun to get the groups to average their individual scores and compare it with the group score.

To facilitate reproduction of the "Guideline Questionnaire" which follows, the answers to the questions are listed here.
Answers: 1. a, 2. a, 3. b, 4. b, 5. f, 6. t, 7. f, 8. f, 9. f, 10. t, 11. f, 12. f, 13.f, 14. f, 15. t, 16. f, 17. f, 18. t, 19. t, 20. t, 21. t, 22. t, 23. f

This questionnaire is based upon the guidelines the Office of Child Development has established for its schools and sponsoring agencies.

Guideline Questionnaire

1. When the OCD Guidelines indicate that something MUST be done:
    a. it is an absolute requirement.
    b. it should be done unless the school Director has a better plan.
    c. only the Policy Group can approve doing it differently.

2. On a Classroom Committee there MUST be:
    a. current parents only.
    b. 50% current parents plus ex-parents.
    c. 50% current parents plus "Representatives of the Community."

3. How is the size (number of members) for a policy group determined?
    a. according to OCD guidelines.
    b. the agency board decides with policy group approval.
    c. the policy group decides.

4. The maximum term of membership allowed as a member of a Child Development policy group is:
    a. one year
    b. three years
    c. as long as the person is doing a good job.

(True - False. Circle the correct answer.)

5. Parents can only be on a policy group by being elected by a joint meeting of parents, staff and Board. T F

6. Child Development staff may attend meetings of policy groups whenever the staff member is interested. T F

7. When a parent is working as a paid aide in the school, he or she is eligible to serve on the policy group as long as her child is in the program. T F

8. Ex-Parents are eligible for positions designated for parents. T F

9. "Representatives of the Community" are designated by the school director to serve as members of the policy group. T F

10. Every school must have a Coordinator of Parent Activities. T F

11. There must be a representative of the Board on the top level Parent Involvement Council policy group. **T F**

12. There must be a representative of the top level Parent Involvement Council policy group on the sponsoring agency's Executive Board. **T F**

13. Home visits by teachers, aides or other staff are requirements which must be accepted by parents of children in the program. **T F**

14. Parents of children in the program are required to visit the classroom and serve as volunteers. **T F**

15. Child Development Centers should set aside space to be used by parents for meetings. **T F**

16. Funds for Parent Activities cannot be provided through the regular school grant or contract. **T F**

17. Approval from the Parent Involvement Council must be secured before a school can determine the location of centers or classes. **T F**

18. Approval from the Parent Involvement Council must be secured before a school can designate delegate agencies. **T F**

19. Approval from the Classroom Committee must be secured before a school can establish criteria for selecting children. **T F**

20. Approval from the Parent Invovlement Council must be secured before a school program can request funds or make major changes in the budget. **T F**

21. Approval from the Policy Committee must be secured before a Delegate Agency can hire or fire Child Development staff. **T F**

22. Approval from the Policy Council must be secured before a school can establish personnel policies or hiring, firing, career development and grievance procedures. **T F**

23. Approval from the Policy Council must be secured before a school can direct the staff in day-to-day operations. **T F**

Day two:

Time: 9:00 a.m.
Objective: Learn Cooperation Between Groups
Methodology: Briefly review the first day and remind the group that the last event was a session on the guidelines. Explain that you will start the second day with a simulation. De-emphasize the notion of "game"; instead, tell the group that they're going to participate in an exercise which will simulate a real-life situation.

The exercise is called the "nickel auction." Divide the total group into two, three or four smaller groups. Each group can have as many as ten members. Next, each group is asked to select a representative and collect all the pennies from each member. With the pennies as his or her "money," the representative will attend an auction where nickels will be sold to the highest bidder. The bidding will start at one penny.

The object of the game is to win as much as possible. After several "auctions," allow the representatives to return to their groups for input about strategy and tactics. After you have auctioned ten nickels, stop the game and discuss what has been learned. Some questions you might ask are:

Who won?
What were the rules for your team?
Did the group representative really represent the group?
What assumptions did you make?
What competition really took place?
How could each have gotten more?

This discussion will point out that the only way to "win" is for each of the players to cooperate very closely. They need to band together so that each person gets a chance to "buy" the nickel for one penny. If the representatives from each group cooperate, they can develop ways to buy nickels for one cent each. You can then make comparisons to the way boards operate and to get the groups to suggest ways in which both Boards can win by "collaboration."

Note: If there is time and it is a receptive group, you may want to try a variation of this game. See Appendix A, "The Prisoner's Dilemma" game. This is a highly successful way to dramatize the natural inclination of different groups to compete with and mistrust one another. It is an excellent exercise to use to train groups about ways to work more closely with one another.

Time: 10:00 a.m. - 12:00 p.m.
Objective: Learn About the Ways and Means of Inter-group Cooperation
Methodology: Participants return to groups with all the Board members in one groups and the Parent Involvement Council members in the other. Ask these two groups to list all the problems and experiences they have had or think exist in the school and in its relationship to the Board.

When the groups have completed their lists, bring them into a large group. You should then help the two groups to see if the items on their lists fall into either of the following categories:

1. Program Operation
2. Policy Issues

As you or individual group members suggest one of these categories for their items, you can add clarifying comments and ask additional questions. Be sure that all issues are raised and understood.

Time: 1:30 p.m. - 3:30 p.m.
Objective: To Develop Recommendations for Collaboration
Methodology: Ask the participants to select a category that interests them and to join a group which will work on that category. (Two groups of roughly the same size should form.) Ask the groups to go through each item on the large group's final list and develop ways to solve or lessen each problem chosen in its category. Later, have the group present its recommendations for solutions or alternatives. If the group can reach any agreement about a solution, record it on a separate large sheet entitled: "Solved Problem List."

Time: 3:30 p.m. - 4:30 p.m.
Objective: Each Group Will Prepare a Strategy Addressing the Question: "Where do we go from here?"
Methodology: Allow each Board group thirty to forty minutes to meet separately to prepare its strategy. When they have finished, ask them to come together and share their final product. Allow for a short discussion and question and answer period.

Time: 4:30 p.m.
Objective: To Conclude the Session
Methodology: Conclude the session by once again having each member draw a picture of him or herself and a one-word description of his or her current mood. Again have them pass the pictures around the room.

(Note: If the participants seem very tired, discouraged, or otherwise down, you should probably just skip this and spend a few minutes congratulating the participants for giving up their time and for working so hard.)

Chapter X
Help, Hints and Concluding Thoughts

ABOUT PARENT INVOLVEMENT

A good parent involvement program is a little like a rich stew. It's made up of many parts and ideas. As it cooks or develops, it changes in color, texture and taste. You might not be sure of exactly what's in it, but nearly everything you add makes it a little better.

That's the trick to having successful parent involvement. Don't let it "dry up" from lack of attention or new ideas and experiments. Keep stirring it with new approaches, new programs, and new ways to help and involve parents. What do we mean by new ideas? What kinds of new approaches and programs?

In this manual you've worked hard to learn a system for organizing parents. You have seen how to construct a vehicle for helping parents have a voice in the program and contribute to it. Remember the example of the woman who wanted to go to the supermarket but had no car? You have now helped to build your own "car" for parent involvement.

Where do you go now? One school in the west developed an "idea bank" for the parent involvement. It took several large pieces of newsprint paper and pasted them to a wall. Whenever anyone had a new idea or a fun way to involve parents, they would write the ideas down on the "Idea Bank" list. Maybe they called it a "Bank" because it was just like putting ideas in a savings account. Here is what it looked like:

Idea Bank

Sewing Bee:
Saturday party to make materials for the center.
Children's Skits:
Children put on little skits; brings parents to the Center for Parent Program. (Be sure to hold parents session first.)
Construction Projects:
Fathers and mothers participate in construction projects, e.g. building a model play-

ground.
Hobby Demonstrations:
Parents and other interested parties demonstrate their hobbies, e.g. woodworking, knitting, glass making, model airplanes, etc.
Field Trips:
Parents take children to places of special interest.
Special uses of Parent Fund for special projects.
Etc.

As you and your Classroom Committee start saving ideas, perhaps you'll find that your list grows and becomes more interesting. Staff, parents, and students will have good ideas. You might even start a prize for the "Best Idea of the Month" for parent involvement.

Another approach you might find helpful is to periodically evaluate your Parent Involvement Program. There are unlimited ways to accomplish this. Spend a few days calling parents and asking them what they think about it. Ask the staff. Suggest it to the Chairperson of each of the program's Classroom Comittee as an agenda item for the next Committee meeting. Better yet, see if you can persuade each Committee to take responsibility for an evaluation of the Parent Involvement Program.

With luck, it will never end. You, your school, and the parents will continue to find new and better ways for the parents to serve as true partners in their children's educational growth.

Appendix A

PRISONER'S DILEMMA GAME

Goals
1. To explore the trust between group members and the effects of trust betrayal.
2. To demonstrate the effect of interpersonal competition.
3. To explain the merit of a collaborative posture in intra-and inter-group relations.

Group Size
Two teams of no more than eight members each.

Time Required
Approximately one hour. Small teams take less time.

Materials Utilized
Prisoners Dilemma Tally Sheets

Physical Setting
There should be enough space for the two teams to meet separately without interrupting or disrupting each other. In the center of the room two chairs for team representatives are place facing each other.

Process
1. The facilitator explains that the group is going to experience a simulation of an old technique used in interrogating prisoners. (He carefully avoids discussing the objectives of the exercise.) The questioner separates prisoners suspected of working together and tells one that the other has confessed and that if they both confess, they will get off easier. The prisoner's dilemma is that they may confess when they should not and that they may fail to confess when they really should.

2. Two teams are formed and seated separately. They are instructed not to communicate with the other team in any way, verbally or non-verbally, except when told to do so by the facilitator.

3. Prisoner's Dilemma Tally Sheets are distributed to all participants. The facilitator

explains that there will be ten rounds of choice, with the Red Team choosing A or B and the Blue Team choosing either X or Y.

AX - Both teams win three points.
AY - Red Team loses 6 point, Blue Team wins 6 points.
BX - Red Team wins 6 points, Blue Team loses 6 points.
BY - Both teams lose three points.

4. Round One is begun, with teams having three minutes in each round to make a decision. The facilitator instructs them not to write down their decision until he signals to do so, to make sure that teams do not make hasty decisions.

5. The choices of the two teams are announced for Round One and the scoring for that round is agreed upon. Rounds 2 and 3 proceed the same way.

6. Round four is announced as special round, with the points payoff doubled. Teams are instructed to send on representative to the center to talk before Round 4. After three minutes of consultation with each other, they return to their teams and round 4 begins. The number of payoff points for the outcome of the round is doubled.

7. Rounds 5 - 8 proceed as in the first three rounds.

8. Round 9 is announced as a special round, with the payoff points squared. Representatives meet for three minutes, and then the teams meet for five minutes. At the facilitator's signal the mark down their choices, and then the two choices are announced. The number of points awarded to the two teams for this round is squared.

9. Round 10 is handled exactly as Round 9. Payoff points are squared.

10. The entire group meets to process the experience. The point total for each team is announced, and the sum of the two outcomes is calculated and compared to the maximum positive outcome. The facilitator may wish to lead a discussion on the effects of high and low trust on their personal relations, on win-lose situations, on zero-sum games, and on the relative merits of collaboration vs. competition.

Prisoner's Dilemma Tally Sheet

Appendix B

Sample By-Laws for a Parent Involvement Council:
A Guide for Revising and Developing By-Laws

The points contained in these By-Laws should be discussed thoroughly with the Board or its representatives.

Article I: Name
The name of this organization shall be the ____ Parent Involvement Council.

Article II: Purposes and Functions
Section 1
The purpose shall be to serve as a link between public and private organizations, the Board, the communities served and the parents of children enrolled in the planning and coordinating of the _____ school.

Section 2
The functions of the ___ Parent Involvement Council are:
1. Initiate suggestions and ideas for program improvements, and to receive periodic reports on action taken by the administering agency with regard to its recommendations.
2. Plan, coordinate and organize agency-wide activities for parents with the assistance of the staff.
3. Administer the Parent Activity Fund.
4. Recruit volunteer services from parents, community residents, and community organizations; and mobilize community resources to meet identified needs.
5. Communicate with all parents and encourage their full participation in the school.
6. Approve the goals for the school within the agency as proposed by the School Board; and develop ways to meet these goals according to program guidelines.
7. Assist in the developing of a plan for recruitment of eligible children and approve such plan.
8. Approve the composition of the appropriate parent policy making groups and methods for setting them up within program guidelines.
9. Approve the services provided to the School.
10. Parent Involvement Council will serve as an intermediary or group that assists or attempts to resolve complaints about the school.

11. Be consulted to ensure that the standards for acquiring space, equipment and supplies are met.
12. Be consulted in the direction of the school staff in the day to day operations.
13. Approve or disapprove the school personnel procedures.
14. Approve the hiring and/or firing of the school Director.
15. Approve or disapprove the hiring and/or firing of the school staff.
16. Approve or disapprove the request for funds and proposed work programs in a timely manner.
17. Approve or disapprove major changes in the school's operating budget and work program while the program is in operation.
18. Conduct a self-evaluation of the school.

Article III
Membership
Section 1
The Parent Involvement Council should be composed of members, with at least 50 percent of the membership comprised of parents of a child currently enrolled in school.

Section 2
Two Categories
Membership on this Parent Involvement Council shall consist of two (2) categories: parent members and community representatives.
a. Each school with 1-2 units is eligible to elect one parent member to the Parent Involvement Council. Parents with a child currently enrolled in that Unit(s) will elect by the quorum stated in their Center By-Laws, a parent of a child currently enrolled in that unit(s) to serve on the Parent Involvement Council.
b. All community representatives must be approved by the parent members of the Parent Involvement Council before they can be seated. Community representatives shall represent major agencies of the communities and counties served by the school.

Section 3
Term of Office
Parent Involvement Council members shall serve for a term of one (1) year. No member shall serve on the Council as a parent member and/or community representative for more that three (3) consecutive years.

Section 4
Voting Rights
Each member of the Parent Involvement Council shall have one (1) vote. There shall

be no proxy voting by, or for, any member.

Section 5
Termination of Membership
A member of the Parent Involvement Council can be terminated by a two-thirds vote of the Council if he is absent from three (3) consecutive meetings without having submitted a legitimate excuse in writing to the Council Chairman (or in his absence the Vice-Chairman) prior to the meeting.

Section 6
Resignation
A member shall give a written statements of reasons before resigning.

Section 7
Vacancy
Any unit(s) shall elect within thirty (3) days a new parent member to the Parent Involvement Council whenever there is a vacancy on the Council occurring at that Unit(s). Of a vacancy occurs from a community representative, the parent members must approve any replacement.

Section 8
Duties
All members of this Parent Involvement Council should attend meetings regularly; arrive on time for all Council and committee meetings; actively participate in meetings by reading the agenda prior to the meeting and discussing matters to be considered with other parents in the unit(s) he represents; keep informed of the Parent Involvement Council's purpose, plans and progress; report back to the parents in the unit(s) he represents any action taken by the Council; remembers the rights of other member to express their opinions; consider all information and arguments before voting; remembering the parents he represents; debate the issues, not person; and accept and support any final decisions of the majority of the Parent Involvement Council.

Article IV
Officers
Section 1
The Parent Involvement Council shall elect a Chairman and Secretary.
Other officers shall be a Vice-Chairman, Treasurer, and other officers as deemed necessary.

Section 2
Election and Term of Office

Each officer shall be elected by the full membership of the Parent Involvement Council once the full Council has been seated and shall serve a term of one (1) year.

Section 3
Removal
Any officer or member of this Parent Involvement Council who fails to perform his duties as outlined above or below, can be removed by a two-thirds vote of the Council.

Section 4
Chairman
The Chairman shall preside at all meetings; talk no more than necessary when presiding; have an understanding of the By-Laws of the Parent Involvement Council; refrain from entering into debates of questions before assembly; shall extend every courtesy to the discussions of the motions; shall call meetings to order and formally close them; note whether a quorum is present and declaration of same; prepare an agenda for each regular meeting and mail it to each member with notice of each regular meeting; shall call special meetings and mail notices of special meetings and explanations of same to each member; appoint chairman to all committees; explain each motion before it is voted upon; and may vote to break a tie.

Section 5
Vice-Chairman
The Vice-Chairman shall preside in the absence of the Chairman or whenever the Chairman temporarily vacates the chair; in case of resignation or death of the Chairman, the Vice-Chairman shall assume the Office of Chairman until a permanent Chairman is elected.

Section 6
Secretary
The Secretary shall record the minutes of every Parent Involvement Council meeting once the meeting has been called to order; keep a copy of the By-Laws, standing rules, list of member, a list of unfinished business and a copy of the agenda; mail copies of the minutes to each Council member in advance if the meeting; see that record of the minutes is kept on file in the office; and receives and handles all mail addressed to the Parent Involvement Council.

Section 7
Treasurer
The Treasurer shall keep an accurate record of the Policy Council's checking account as to all money received and/or spent; signs all checks; and makes regular reports to the Policy Council of all expenditures relating to the administration of the Parent

Activity Fund and any other funds or moneys received and disbursed.

Article V
Committees
Section 1
The Parent Involvement Council shall appoint such committees as are necessary to the proper conduct of its business, including but not limited to the following: Executive Committee, Personnel Committee, Grievance Committee, and Finance Committee.

Section 2
Executive Committee
The Executive Committee shall be composed of the Offices of this Parent Involvement Council. This Executive Committee shall have the power to conduct business for the Parent Involvement Council between regular meetings of the Council.

Section 3
Grievance Committee
As stipulated in the functions of this Parent Involvement Council, this committee shall hear the grievances from the community, and from parents who have followed the grievance procedures at the center level, about the school; and make recommendations to the Council to resolve these complaints. This committee may also hear grievances of school staff and present their findings to the Personnel Committee or School Board Of Directors.

Section 4
Personnel Committee
As stipulated in the functions of this Parent Involvement Council, this committee will discuss the school personnel policies and procedures and make recommendations to the Parent Involvement Council prior to the Council's approving said personnel policies and procedures. This committee will also screen, interview and recommend persons to be hired to fill vacancies in the school staff.

Section 5
Finance Committee
As stipulated in the functions of this Parent Involvement Council, this committee will prepare the budget for the Parent Activity Fund for approval of the Council before being submitted to any higher committee; and recommends to the Parent Involvement Council how to administer the Parent Activity Fund and approve expenditures by the Treasurer.

Section 6

Special Committees
Special Committees may be appointed by the Chairman or selected by the Parent Involvement Council as the need arises.

Article VI
Meetings
Section 1
Regular Meetings
Regular meetings of this Parent Involvement Council will be held once a month.

Section 2
Special Meetings
There will be special meetings of this Parent Involvement Council only when the Council sees a need, and all special meetings shall be called by the Chairman at least forty-eight (48) hours in advance.

Section 3
Notice of Meetings
Written notices shall be mailed to each Parent Involvement Council member by the Chairman at least forty-eight (48) hours prior to the date of the meeting with an explanation for calling the special meeting. Follow-up phone calls by the Secretary may be in order.

Section 4
Quorum
A majority of the members of this Parent Involvement Council must be present to constitute a quorum for regular or special meetings to transact business.

Article VII
Amendments
These By-Laws may be amended by sending a copy of the proposed amendment to each Parent Involvement Council member at least one (1) week before the meeting. The Council may debate an amendment before adoption. Amendments must be approved by a two-thirds vote of the Parent Involvement Council.

Chairman, Board of Directors

Chairman, Parent Involvement Council

Points to consider in preparing by-laws for your agency:

Meetings open to the public
What method of parliamentary procedure shall be followed?
What about parent member alternates?
What about compensation for poverty-level parent members travel and baby-sitting?
Should a nominating committee be named to draw up a slate of officers?
What is the membership of standing committees?
How are vacancies on committees filled?

www.ingramcontent.com/pod-product-compliance
Lightning Source LLC
Chambersburg PA
CBHW081135170426
43197CB00017B/2865